Books by Clifford McCarty

1953 *Film Composers in America: A Checklist of Their Work*
1955 *Music and Recordings, 1955*
     (with Frederic V. Grunfeld, *et al.*)
1965 *Bogey: The Films of Humphrey Bogart*
1969 *The Films of Errol Flynn*
     (with Tony Thomas and Rudy Behlmer)
1971 *Published Screenplays: A Checklist*

Published Screenplays

A Checklist

By Clifford McCarty

The Kent State University Press

The Serif Series:
Bibliographies and Checklists, Number 18
William White, General Editor
Wayne State University

For Max

Introduction

It has been said that D. W. Griffith, the screen's first genius, filmed *Intolerance* from his own concept and without a written script. Perhaps. Only a genius could do it, or should even attempt it. Dudley Nichols, one of the screen's most gifted writers, maintained that the screenplay, though "not a completed thing in itself," is the "first [and] most important stage in the creation of a film."

Like the other components of a motion picture, the screenplay is usually available only on film. Outside of the theater, the screenplay, except for what can be recalled by memory, becomes inaccessible. Occasionally, of course, screenplays are published, as they have been almost from the motion picture's inception, though not until the late Twenties for any but utilitarian reasons. Edwin S. Porter's scenario for *Life of an American Fireman* was published in the Edison Catalogue of 1903, doubtlessly to help sell the film to exhibitors. Most of the scenarios published during the next quarter-century were included in screenwriting manuals intended for would-be scenarists. Although there is no evidence that these textbooks helped anyone become a professional screenwriter, there seems reason to credit them with inspiring some of the many privately printed but unfilmed scenarios, frequently on religious or patriotic themes, that appeared during the first three decades of this century.[1]

The first anthology of screenplays, *Motion Picture Continuities*, was published in 1929, and though the scripts were offered as practical examples for prospective screenwriters, there was also the suggestion that they could be enjoyed as a literary form. In 1934 Covici-Friede published *The Mighty Barnum*, the first screenplay of an American sound film to be issued in book form, and Methuen published *The Private Life of Henry VIII*, the first complete script of a British film in book form. The following year Methuen also published the script of *Jew Süss*, but there apparently was insufficient public interest in the form, and what seemed to be an incipient series expired with the second volume. Several other screenplays, however, appeared during the next few years, and by 1943, when Crown Publishers issued *Twenty Best Film Plays*, critic John Gassner was able to announce in his introduction that "there is now a literature of the screen—the screenplay." This important collection (and the largest to appear before or since) was followed by two annuals, but, as with the Methuen volumes, the projected series came to an end.

In the Sixties, with an increase in the publication of all types of film books, screenplays proliferated. Yet after seven decades and all the bustle of recent years, only a relative handful of screenplays is available in reading form. Publication has been fitful and sometimes seemingly capricious. The producers themselves have shown no interest in issuing scripts; *In Old Chicago* is unique in being the only screenplay published by a film studio. The script for *Trio*, an English film, was published

---

[1] These are excluded here, since they have no importance as either cinema or literature. Some are listed on pp. 276–279 of *The Film Index* (New York: The Museum of Modern Art Film Library and The H. W. Wilson Company, 1941; New York: Arno Press for the Museum of Modern Art, 1966).

only in America, while the script for *Judgment at Nuremberg*,
an American film, was published only in England. Erich von
Stroheim's scenario for *Greed*, an American release of 1924, was
finally published in 1958—in Belgium! The current series of
scripts published by Lorrimer in England and by Simon and
Schuster in this country, now numbering seventeen volumes,
does not include a single American screenplay. Perhaps
permission to publish such scripts has been denied—Gassner
speaks of this difficulty in compiling his three collections—but
it is hard to believe that some enterprising publisher could
not wheedle from the owners the rights to publish, say, *Citizen
Kane* or *The Treasure of the Sierra Madre*.

A large number of screenplays have appeared only in paper-
back editions—not just quality paperbacks such as the Lorrimer
series, but mass-market paperbacks, which because of their
cheap manufacture are usually short-lived. It is worth noting
that these inexpensive paperbacks have constituted the sole
publication of screenplays by Bernard Shaw, Christopher Fry,
Terence Rattigan, William Inge, Paddy Chayefsky, and
William Goldman. Mass-market paperbacks usually are not
listed in such references as the *Cumulative Book Index*,
and to record these ephemeral publications is one purpose of
this checklist. Another purpose is to locate scripts where
their presence may go unnoticed: in writers' handbooks, bi-
ographies and autobiographies, monographs on directors,
anthologies, periodicals, and books on film history, aesthetics,
and technique.

In the case of produced screenplays, this checklist is intended
to be inclusive rather than selective; therefore, not only complete
screenplays are included but excerpts as well. The "literature
of the screen" is not so exhaustive that fragments can be
overlooked. Very brief extracts of only a few lines have been
omitted, but any excerpt of one page or more has been thought

sufficient for inclusion. In the case of unproduced screenplays, only those by professional film-makers, and those written by, or based upon works by, figures of some literary reputation have been admitted.

Other forms of film-writing such as outlines, synopses, and "treatments," as well as most novels, whether those upon which screenplays have been based or those themselves based on screenplays, have been excluded. Exceptions have been made in the case of the "film-novel," such as H. G. Wells' *Man Who Could Work Miracles* and Arthur Miller's *The Misfits*, and in the case of "screenplays in reading form," the designation given the Stein and Day series which includes *America America* and *The Swimmer*. I have also been less exacting about the scenarios of *avant-garde* films, since they are by nature unconventional.

All types of films are represented: features, shorts, documentaries, experimental films—even an animated cartoon. The only requirements are that the screenplay be published in English and issued commercially. Mimeographed studio scripts and screenplays published in foreign languages are not listed.[2]

The screenplays in this checklist are arranged alphabetically by title. Articles (*a*, *an*, *the*, and their foreign equivalents) are ignored. The following is a sample entry:

(1) *Casablanca*
(2) Warner Bros., 1943.
(3) Directed by Michael Curtiz.
(4) Screenplay by Julius J. Epstein, Philip G. Epstein and Howard Koch.

---

[2] Many of these will be found in the Italian bibliography, *Soggetti e Sceneggiature*, edited by Davide Turconi and Camillo Bassotto (Venice: Edizioni Mostra Cinema, 1967).

(5) Based on the play *Everybody Comes to Rick's* by Murray Burnett and Joan Alison.

(6) *Best Film Plays of 1943–1944*, edited by John Gassner and Dudley Nichols. New York: Crown Publishers, 1945, pp. 631–694.

Although such an entry seems self-explanatory, the variations in entries warrant a few words of amplification:

(1) *The title of the film.* Foreign films are listed under their published titles. If the published title is in English, the original title is given in parentheses, e.g., *Last Year at Marienbad* (*L'Année Dernière à Marienbad*). If the published title is foreign, an English-language title is given in parentheses if the film was shown here under that title, if the translation appears in the published script, or if the translation is commonly used in writings about the film. When a foreign film is known only by its original title, e.g., *La Strada*, no translation is provided. All alternate titles are listed in the index. Where it is stated that a script was *produced under another title*, this information comes from the book in which the script was published, and where the failure to identify the release title is unexplained. Omnibus films such as *Quartet* and *Trio*, if published in their entirety, appear under their main titles, with the titles of their individual episodes listed in the index. Episodes published separately appear under the part title, with the film's main title listed in the index.

(2) *The film's production company and date.* For American films, the date is that of copyright; for foreign films, that of first public showing. Films other than features are identified as *short, documentary*, etc. *Unproduced* indicates a screenplay that has not been filmed.

(3) *The director of the film.* He is listed here since he is

often considered to be the "author" of a film, though it will be seen that his name does not always appear under (4).

(4)   *The author(s) of the screenplay.* Sometimes the names are different from those on the published screenplay, and in such cases are more accurate than the published names. In a few entries the names of additional contributors appear in parentheses; these are writers who contributed ten percent or more of the screenplay but because of studio policy received no screen credit. *Original screenplay* indicates one written directly for the screen and not based on a previous work. I have arbitrarily used *scenario* for the script of a silent film, *screenplay* for the script of a sound film.

Some dates, directors, and screenwriters have been omitted when they could not be identified.

(5)   *The source of the screenplay* (if not original), i.e., the novel, play, book, or story upon which the screenplay is based, and it's author(s). *Original story* indicates one written expressly for the film and not previously published.

(6)   *The location of the published screenplay,* giving title, author or editor, place of publication, publisher, date, and pagination. For a screenplay published separately, the pagination is that of the entire book. For a screenplay not published separately, the pages given are those on which the screenplay appears. Screenplays not published in their entirety are marked *excerpt(s).* When a screenplay has been published more than once, complete scripts are listed first, in chronological order, followed by excerpts, also listed chronologically.

For facilitating my research I am grateful to the staffs of the Los Angeles Public Library, the University of Southern California Library, the Libraries of the University of California at Los Angeles, and the Library of the Academy of Motion

Picture Arts and Sciences. I especially thank Mildred Simpson, Librarian of the Academy, for her many valuable suggestions and for her counsel on certain bibliographical details; Mr. and Mrs. Milton Luboviski of Larry Edmunds Bookshop for allowing me to roam at will through their large stock; DeWitt Bodeen for information drawn from his many years as a screenwriter and film historian; and Lloyd Phillip Cohn for calling my attention to several published screenplays that escaped my notice. These kind people, though responsible for many inclusions in this book, are in no way liable for any omissions or errors, which are due entirely to my own ignorance. Additions and corrections are warmly solicited.

CLIFFORD McCARTY

Los Angeles
October 1970

Published Screenplays

1 *Across the Great Divide*
Edison, 1915 (short).
Directed by Edward C. Taylor.
Scenario by Edward C. Taylor.
Based on the story "With Clear Rights" by Charles W. Tyler.
A-B-C of Motion Pictures, by Robert E. Welsh. New York:
  Harper & Brothers, 1916, pp. 96–107.

2 *Adventure—Balloon to Serengeti*
B. B. C., 196? (documentary short).
A Film Maker's Guide, by Brian Branston. London: George
  Allen & Unwin, 1967, pp. 129–132, 136–161 (excerpts).

3 *The Adventures of Marco Polo*
Samuel Goldwyn/United Artists, 1938.
Directed by Archie Mayo.
Screenplay by Robert E. Sherwood.
Based on an original story by N. A. Pogson.
How to Write and Sell Film Stories, by Frances Marion. New
  York: Covici-Friede, 1937, pp. 231–364.

4 *The Adventures of Tom Sawyer*
Selznick International/United Artists, 1938.
Directed by Norman Taurog.
Screenplay by John V. A. Weaver.
Continuity by Barbara Keon.
(Contributor to treatment: Marshall Neilan.)
Based on the novel by Mark Twain (pseud. of Samuel L.
Clemens).
The Moving Image, by Robert Gessner. New York: E. P.
Dutton & Co., 1968, pp. 276–277 (excerpt).

5 *The African Queen*
Romulus-Horizon/United Artists, 1951.
Directed by John Huston.
Screenplay by James Agee and John Huston.
Based on the novel by C. S. Forester.
Agee on Film, Volume Two, by James Agee. New York:
McDowell, Obolensky, 1960, pp. 149–259. Boston: Beacon
Press, 1964, pp. 149–259. New York: Grosset & Dunlap,
1969, pp. 149–259.

6 *L'Âge d'Or* (*The Golden Age*)
Charles de Noailles, 1930.
Directed by Luis Buñuel.
Original scenario by Luis Buñuel and Salvador Dali.
L'Age d'Or and Un Chien Andalou, by Luis Buñuel. London:
Lorrimer Publishing ,1968, pp. 15–71. New York: Simon
and Schuster, 1968, pp. 15–71.
Luis Buñuel, by Ado Kyrou. New York: Simon and Schuster,
1963, pp. 151–159 (excerpts).

7   *Alexander Nevsky*
Mosfilm, 1938.
Directed by Sergei M. Eisenstein and Dmitri Vasiliev.
Original screenplay by Pyotr Pavlenko and Sergei M. Eisenstein.
The Moving Image, by Robert Gessner. New York: E. P.
    Dutton & Co., 1968, pp. 194–195 (excerpts).
Sergei Eisenstein, by Léon Moussinac. New York: Crown
    Publishers, 1970, pp. 142–145 (excerpt).

8   *Algiers*
Walter Wanger/United Artists, 1938.
Directed by John Cromwell.
Screenplay by John Howard Lawson.
Additional dialogue by James M. Cain.
Based on the novel *Pépé le Moko* by Detective Ashelbe (pseud.
    of Henri La Barthe).
Foremost Films of 1938, by Frank Vreeland. New York and
    Chicago: Pitman Publishing Corporation, 1939, pp. 97–113
    (excerpts).

9   *All About Eve*
Twentieth Century-Fox, 1950.
Directed by Joseph L. Mankiewicz.
Screenplay by Joseph L. Mankiewicz.
Based on the story "The Wisdom of Eve" by Mary Orr.
All About Eve, by Joseph L. Mankiewicz. New York: Random
    House, 1951, 245 pp.
The Moving Image, by Robert Gessner. New York: E. P.
    Dutton & Co., 1968, pp. 80–83 (excerpt).

10   *All Quiet on the Western Front*
Universal, 1930.

Directed by Lewis Milestone.
Screenplay by Maxwell Anderson and George Abbott.
Adaptation by Del Andrews.
Based on the novel by Erich Maria Remarque.
Experimental Cinema, I, No. 2 (June 1930), 23–27 (proposed
but unaccepted ending by Werner Klinger).

11 *All That Money Can Buy*
RKO Radio, 1941.
Directed by William Dieterle.
Screenplay by Dan Totheroh and Stephen Vincent Benét.
Based on the story "The Devil and Daniel Webster" by Stephen
Vincent Benét.
Twenty Best Film Plays, edited by John Gassner and Dudley
Nichols. New York: Crown Publishers, 1943, pp. 951–994.
Great Film Plays, edited by John Gassner and Dudley Nichols.
New York: Crown Publishers, 1959, pp. 247–290.

12 *All the Way Home*
Talent Associates/Paramount, 1963.
Directed by Alex Segal.
Screenplay by Philip Reisman, Jr.
Based on the play *All the Way Home* by Tad Mosel, and the
novel *A Death in the Family* by James Agee.
All the Way Home, by Tad Mosel and Philip Reisman, Jr.
New York: Avon Books, 1963, 365 pp. (includes the text of
the stage play).

13 *Alphaville*
Chaumiane-Filmstudio, 1965.
Directed by Jean-Luc Godard.
Original screenplay by Jean-Luc Godard.

Alphaville, by Jean-Luc Godard. London: Lorrimer Films, 1966, 102 pp. New York: Simon and Schuster, 1968, 102 pp.
Jean-Luc Godard, by Jean Collet. New York: Crown Publishers, 1970, pp. 132–135 (excerpts).

14 *America America*
Athena Enterprises/Warner Bros., 1963.
Directed by Elia Kazan.
Screenplay by Elia Kazan, based on his book.
America America, by Elia Kazan. New York: Stein and Day, 1962, 190 pp.

15 *An American Tragedy*
Unproduced.
Scenario by Sergei M. Eisenstein, Grigori Alexandrov and Ivor Montagu.
Based on the novel by Theodore Dreiser.
(Another version, scripted by Samuel Hoffenstein, was filmed in 1931. Still another version, scripted by Michael Wilson and Harry Brown, was filmed in 1951 as *A Place in the Sun*.)
With Eisenstein in Hollywood, by Ivor Montagu. New York: International Publishers, 1969, pp. 207–341.
The Film Sense, by Sergei M. Eisenstein. New York: Harcourt, Brace and Company, 1942, pp. 236–242 (excerpt).

16 *Americans All!* (*The March of Time*, Vol. 7, No. 7)
Time, Inc./RKO Radio, 1941 (documentary short).
Of the People, edited by Harry R. Warfel and Elizabeth W. Manwaring. New York: Oxford University Press, 1942, 15-page section between pp. 340–341.

17   *Le Amiche* (*The Girl Friends*)
Trionfalcine, 1955.
Directed by Michelangelo Antonioni.
Screenplay by Michelangelo Antonioni, Suso Cecchi d'Amico
and Alba de Cespedes.
Based on the story "Tra Donne Sole" ("Among Lonely
Women") by Cesare Pavese.
Michelangelo Antonioni, by Pierre Leprohon. New York:
Simon and Schuster, 1963, pp. 125–131 (excerpt).
Antonioni, by Ian Cameron and Robin Wood. London: Studio
Vista, 1968, pp. 51–58 (excerpts). New York: Frederick
A. Praeger, 1969, pp. 51–58 (excerpts).

18   *Anatahan*
Daiwa, 1953.
Directed by Josef von Sternberg.
Screenplay by Asano.
English narration by Josef von Sternberg.
Based on the novel by Michiro Maruyama.
Josef von Sternberg, by Herman G. Weinberg. New York:
E. P. Dutton & Co., 1967, pp. 163–175 (English narration
only).

19   *Anna Karenina*
Metro-Goldwyn-Mayer, 1935.
Directed by Clarence Brown.
Screenplay by Clemence Dane and Salka Viertel.
Dialogue adaptation by S. N. Behrman.
Based on the novel by Leo Tolstoy.
The Moving Image, by Robert Gessner. New York: E. P.
Dutton & Co., 1968, pp. 120–121, 318–319, 383–384
(excerpts).

20 *Anna Karenina*
London Films, 1948.
Directed by Julien Duvivier.
Screenplay by Jean Anouilh, Guy Morgan and Julien Duvivier.
Based on the novel by Leo Tolstoy.
Film Script, by Adrian Brunel. London: Burke Publishing
Company, 1948, pp. 164–170 (excerpt).

21 *Archie and the Bell-Boy*
Edison, 1913 (short).
Directed by C. Jay Williams.
Original scenario by Alice Williams.
The Motion Picture Story, by William Lord Wright. Chicago:
Cloud Publishing Company, 1914, pp. 141–160.

22 *Arms and the Man*
Unproduced.
Screenplay by Bernard Shaw, based on his play.
The Serpent's Eye, by Donald P. Costello. Notre Dame:
University of Notre Dame Press, 1965, pp. 189–196.

23 *Army in Action*
U. S. Army Pictorial Center, 1965 (series of 13 documentary
shorts).
Scripts and direction by Norton S. Parker.
Audiovisual Script Writing, by Norton S. Parker. New
Brunswick: Rutgers University Press, 1968, pp. 204-291
(Episode 1: "Winds of Change"; Episode 2: "The Three
Faces of Evil"; Episode 3: "Flames on the Horizon";
Episode 13: "The Finest Tradition").

24   *Auntie's Affinity*
Lubin, 1913 (short).
Directed by Barry O'Neil.
Original scenario by Lawrence S. McCloskey.

The Technique of the Photoplay, by Epes Winthrop Sargent.
New York: The Moving Picture World, 1913 (Second
edition), pp. 173–182.

25   *Une Aussi Longue Absence*
Procinex, 1961.
Directed by Henri Colpi.
Original screenplay by Marguerite Duras and Gérard Jarlot.
Hiroshima Mon Amour; Une Aussi Longue Absence, by
Marguerite Duras. London: Calder and Boyars, 1966,
pp. 115–191.

26   *L'Avventura*
Produzioni Cinematografiche Europèe–Société Cinéma-
tographique Lyre, 1960.
Directed by Michelangelo Antonioni.
Screenplay by Michelangelo Antonioni, Elio Bartolini and
Tonino Guerra.
Based on an original story by Michelangelo Antonioni.
Screenplays of Michelangelo Antonioni. New York: The Orion
Press, 1963, pp. 93–208.
L'Avventura, by Michelangelo Antonioni. New York: Grove
Press, 1969, 288 pp.

27   *Babaouo*
Unproduced.
Original scenario by Salvador Dali.
Cinemages, No. 9 (August 1, 1958), pp. 19–28 (excerpts).

28   *Baby Doll*
Newtown/Warner Bros., 1956.
Directed by Elia Kazan.
Original screenplay by Tennessee Williams.
Baby Doll, by Tennessee Williams. New York: New Directions,
  1956, 208 pp. New York: The New American Library
  (Signet Books), 1956, 128 pp. London: Secker & Warburg,
  1957, 140 pp.

29   *Bachelor Mother*
RKO Radio, 1939.
Directed by Garson Kanin.
Screenplay by Norman Krasna.
Based on an original story by Felix Jackson.
The Best Pictures, 1939–1940, edited by Jerry Wald and
  Richard Macaulay. New York: Dodd, Mead & Company,
  1940, pp. 1–29 (excerpts).

30   *The Bachelor Party*
Norma/United Artists, 1957.
Directed by Delbert Mann.
Screenplay by Paddy Chayefsky, based on his teleplay.
The Bachelor Party, by Paddy Chayefsky. New York: The New
  American Library (Signet Books), 1957, 127 pp.

31   *Back Door to Heaven*
Odessco/Paramount, 1939.
Directed by William K. Howard.
Screenplay by John Bright and Robert Tasker.
Based on an original story by William K. Howard.

One Act Play Magazine, II, No. 6 (December 1938), 584–593 (excerpt).
New Fields for the Writer, edited by Stephen Moore. New York: National Library Press, 1939, pp. 73–87 (excerpt).

32   *The Bad Lord Byron*
Gainsborough, 1949.
Directed by David Macdonald.
Original screenplay by Terence Young, Anthony Thorne, Peter Quennell, Laurence Kitchin and Paul Holt.

The Bad Lord Byron, by Sydney Box and Vivian Cox. London: Convoy Publications, 1949, pp. 66–86 (excerpts).

33   *Barabbas*
Dino De Laurentiis/Columbia, 1962.
Directed by Richard Fleischer.
Screenplay by Christopher Fry, assisted by Dieggo Fabbri, Ivo Perilli and Giusèppe Berto.
Based on the novel by Pär Lagerkvist.
Barabbas: The Story of a Motion Picture, edited by Lon Jones. Bologna, Italy: Cappelli, 1962, pp. 75–97, 113–128 (excerpts).

34   *A Battle of Wealth*
Lubin, 19?? (short).
Scenario Writing, by Ernest N. Ross. Philadelphia: Penn Association, 1912, pp. 56–61.

35   *The Battleship Potemkin*
Goskino, 1925.
Directed by Sergei M. Eisenstein.

Scenario by Sergei M. Eisenstein.
Based on an original story by Nina Agadzhanova-Shutko.
The Battleship Potemkin, by Sergei Eisenstein. London:
Lorrimer Publishing, 1968, 100 pp.
Potemkin, by Sergei Eisenstein. New York: Simon and Schuster,
1968, 100 pp.
Sergei Eisenstein, by Léon Moussinac. New York: Crown
Publishers, 1970, pp. 109–122 (excerpts).

36 *The Beach of Falesá*
Unproduced.
Screenplay by Dylan Thomas.
Based on the story by Robert Louis Stevenson.
The Beach of Falesá, by Dylan Thomas. New York: Stein and
Day, 1963, 126 pp. New York: Ballantine Books, 1965,
158 pp.

37 *Beat the Devil*
Santana-Romulus/United Artists, 1954.
Directed by John Huston.
Screenplay by John Huston and Truman Capote.
Based on the novel by James Helvick.
The Moving Image, by Robert Gessner. New York: E. P.
Dutton & Co., 1968, 325–326 (excerpt).

38 *La Beauté du Diable* (*Beauty and the Devil*)
Universalia, 1949.
Directed by René Clair.
Original screenplay by René Clair and Armand Salacrou.
Four Screenplays, by René Clair. New York: The Orion Press,
1970, pp. 113–211.

39   *Les Belles-de-Nuit* (*Beauties of the Night*)
Franco-London Film–Rizzoli Film, 1952.
Directed by René Clair.
Original screenplay by René Clair, assisted by Jean-Pierre
  Grédy and Pierre Barillet.
Four Screenplays, by René Clair. New York: The Orion Press,
  1970, pp. 215–317.

40   *Beyond Recall*
Arrow/Pathé, 1916 (short).
Original scenario by Louis Reeves Harrison.
Screencraft, by Louis Reeves Harrison. New York: Chalmers
  Publishing Co., 1916, pp. 123–141.

41   *The Bible*
Dino De Laurentiis/Twentieth Century-Fox, 1966.
Directed by John Huston.
Screenplay by Christopher Fry, assisted by Jonathan Griffin,
  Ivo Perilli and Vittorio Bonicelli.
Based on the Book of Genesis, Holy Bible.
The Bible, by Christopher Fry. New York: Pocket Books, 1966,
  174 pp.

42   *The Bicycle Thief* (*Ladri di Biciclette*)
Produzioni De Sica, 1949.
Directed by Vittorio De Sica.
Screenplay by Cesare Zavattini.
Dialogue and scene arrangement by Oreste Biancoli, Suso
  Cecchi d'Amico, Vittorio De Sica, Adolfo Franci, Gherardo
  Gherardi, Gerardo Guerrieri and Cesare Zavattini.
English titles by Alfred Hayes.
Based on the novel by Luigi Bartolini.

Bicycle Thieves, by Vittorio De Sica. London: Lorrimer
Publishing, 1968, 96 pp.
The Bicycle Thief, by Vittorio De Sica. New York: Simon and
Schuster, 1968, 96 pp.

43   *Il Bidone (The Swindle)*
Titanus, 1955.
Directed by Federico Fellini.
Screenplay by Federico Fellini, Ennio Flaiano and Tullio
Pinelli.
Based on an original story by Federico Fellini and Ennio Flaiano.
Three Screenplays, by Federico Fellini. New York: The Orion
Press, 1970, pp. 133–252.
Federico Fellini, by Gilbert Salachas. New York: Crown
Publishers, 1969, pp. 132–135 (excerpt).

44   *The Big Sleep*
Warner Bros., 1946.
Directed by Howard Hawks.
Screenplay by William Faulkner, Leigh Brackett and Jules
Furthman.
Based on the novel by Raymond Chandler.
The Moving Image, by Robert Gessner. New York: E. P.
Dutton & Co., 1968, pp. 367–369 (excerpt).

45   *The Birth of a Nation*
Epoch, 1915.
Directed by D. W. Griffith.
Scenario by D. W. Griffith, Frank E. Woods and Thomas
Dixon, Jr.
Based on the novel *The Clansman* by Thomas Dixon, Jr.

A Shot Analysis of D. W. Griffith's The Birth of a Nation, by
   Theodore Huff. New York: The Museum of Modern Art
   Film Library, 1961, 69 pp.
The Rise of the American Film, by Lewis Jacobs. New York:
   Harcourt, Brace and Company, 1939, pp. 180–185 (excerpt).

46 *Blockade*
Walter Wanger/United Artists, 1938.
Directed by William Dieterle.
Original screenplay by John Howard Lawson.
One Act Play Magazine, II, No. 4 (October 1938), 405–420
   (excerpt).

47 *The Blood of a Poet (Le Sang d'un Poète)*
Jean Cocteau, 1930.
Directed by Jean Cocteau.
Original scenario by Jean Cocteau.
The Blood of a Poet, by Jean Cocteau. New York: Bodley Press,
   1949, 53 pp.
Two Screenplays, by Jean Cocteau. New York: The Orion Press,
   1968, pp. 1–60. Baltimore: Penguin Books, 1969, pp. 1–60.
   London: Calder and Boyars, 1970, pp. 1–60.
Jean Cocteau, by René Gilson. New York: Crown Publishers,
   1969, pp. 128–131 (excerpts).

48 *Blossom Time* (U. S. title: *April Romance*)
Alliance Films, 1934.
Directed by Paul L. Stein.
Screenplay, dialogue and lyrics by Franz Schulz, John
   Drinkwater, Roger Burford and G. H. Clutsam.
Based on the life of Franz Schubert.

Money for Film Stories, by Norman Lee. London: Sir Isaac
Pitman & Sons, 1937, p. 146 (excerpt).

49 *The Blue Angel* (*Der Blaue Engel*)
Ufa, 1930.
Directed by Josef von Sternberg.
Screenplay by Robert Liebmann.
Based on the novel *Professor Unrath* by Heinrich Mann.
The Blue Angel, by Josef von Sternberg. London: Lorrimer
Publishing, 1968, 111 pp. New York: Simon and Schuster,
1968, 111 pp.

50 *The Blue Hotel*
Unproduced.
Screenplay by James Agee.
Based on the story by Stephen Crane.
Agee on Film, Volume Two, by James Agee. New York:
McDowell, Obolensky, 1960, pp. 391–488. Boston: Beacon
Press, 1964, pp. 391–488. New York: Grosset & Dunlap,
1969, pp. 391–488.

51 *Blue Movie*
Andy Warhol, 1969.
Directed by Andy Warhol.
Original screenplay by Andy Warhol.
Blue Movie, by Andy Warhol. New York: Grove Press, 1970,
126 pp.

52 *Borrowed Plumes*
Universal-Rex, 1916 (short).

Directed by Ben Wilson.
Original scenario by Helmer W. Bergman.
Photoplay Magazine, X, No. 1 (June 1916), 132–135.

53 *The Bride Comes to Yellow Sky* (Part II of *Face to Face*)
Theasquare/RKO Radio, 1952.
Directed by Bretaigne Windust.
Screenplay by James Agee.
Based on the story by Stephen Crane.
Agee on Film, Volume Two, by James Agee. New York:
   McDowell, Obolensky, 1960, pp. 355–390. Boston: Beacon
   Press, 1964, pp. 355–390. New York: Grosset & Dunlap,
   1969, pp. 355–390.

54 *The Bridge on the River Kwai*
Horizon/Columbia, 1957.
Directed by David Lean.
Screenplay by Pierre Boulle, based on his novel *The Bridge
   Over the River Kwai.*
The Moving Image, by Robert Gessner. New York: E. P.
   Dutton & Co., 1968, pp. 326–327, 382–383 (excerpts).

55 *Brief Encounter*
Cineguild, 1946.
Directed by David Lean.
Screenplay by David Lean, Anthony Havelock-Allan and
   Ronald Neame.
Adaptation by Noel Coward, David Lean and Anthony
   Havelock-Allan.
Based on the one-act play "Still Life" by Noel Coward.
Three British Screen Plays, edited by Roger Manvell. London:
   Methuen & Co., 1950, pp. 1–82.

56   *Broadway*
Universal, 1929.
Directed by Paul Fejos.
Screenplay by Edward T. Lowe, Jr. and Charles Furthman.
Based on the play by Philip Dunning and George Abbott.
Writing the Sound and Dialogue Photoplay, by Tom Terriss.
   Hollywood: Palmer Institute of Authorship, 1930,
   pp. 1-S–41-S (excerpts).

57   *Broken Journey*
Gainsborough, 1948.
Directed by Ken Annakin.
Original screenplay by Robert Westerby.
Film Script, by Adrian Brunel. London: Burke Publishing
   Company, 1948, pp. 171–182 (excerpts).

58   *Brotherhood of Man*
United Productions of America, 1946 (animated short).
Directed by Robert Cannon.
Original screenplay by Ring Lardner, Jr., Maurice Rapf, John
   Hubley and Phil Eastman.
Hollywood Quarterly, I, No. 4 (July 1946), 353–359.

59   *The Buccaneer*
Paramount, 1938.
Directed by Cecil B. DeMille.
Screenplay by Edwin Justus Mayer, Harold Lamb and C.
   Gardner Sullivan.
Adaptation by Jeanie Macpherson.
(Contributor to screenplay construction and dialogue: Grover
   Jones.)
Based on the book *Lafitte the Pirate* by Lyle Saxon.

Foremost Films of 1938, by Frank Vreeland. New York and Chicago: Pitman Publishing Corporation, 1939, pp. 63–78 (excerpts).

60   *Butch Cassidy and the Sundance Kid*
Twentieth Century-Fox, 1969.
Directed by George Roy Hill.
Original screenplay by William Goldman.
Butch Cassidy and the Sundance Kid, by William Goldman. New York: Bantam Books, 1969, 184 pp.

61   *The Cabinet of Dr. Caligari (Das Kabinett des Doktor Caligari)*
Delca-Bioskop, 1919.
Directed by Robert Wiene.
Original scenario by Hans Janowitz and Carl Mayer.
Films of Tyranny, by Richard B. Byrne. Madison, Wisconsin: College Printing & Typing Co., 1966, pp. 1–42 (shot analysis).

62   *The Caine Mutiny*
Stanley Kramer/Columbia, 1954.
Directed by Edward Dmytryk.
Screenplay by Stanley Roberts.
Additional dialogue by Michael Blankfort.
Based on the novel by Herman Wouk.
The Moving Image, by Robert Gessner. New York: E. P. Dutton & Co., 1968, pp. 344–346 (excerpts).

63   *The Call of the Blood*
Universal, 1921 (short).

Directed by Edward Laemmle.
Original scenario by George Morgan.
Photoplay Writing, by William Lord Wright. New York: Falk
Publishing Co., 1922, pp. 67–81.

64   *The Captive Heart*
Ealing Studios, 1946.
Directed by Basil Dearden.
Screenplay by Angus MacPhail and Guy Morgan.
Based on an original story by Patrick Kirwan.
Film Script, by Adrian Brunel. London: Burke Publishing
Company, 1948, pp. 152–163 (excerpts).

65   *Les Carabiniers* (*The Riflemen*)
Rome-Paris Films–Laetitia, 1963.
Directed by Jean-Luc Godard.
Screenplay by Jean-Luc Godard, Roberto Rossellini and Jean
Gruault.
Based on the play *I Carabinieri* by Benjamino Joppolo, adapted
into French by Jacques Audiberti.
Jean-Luc Godard, by Jean Collet. New York: Crown Publishers,
1970, pp. 130–132 (excerpt).

66   *Casablanca*
Warner Bros., 1943.
Directed by Michael Curtiz.
Screenplay by Julius J. Epstein, Philip G. Epstein and Howard
Koch.
Based on the play *Everybody Comes to Rick's* by Murray
Burnett and Joan Alison.

Best Film Plays of 1943–1944, edited by John Gassner and
Dudley Nichols. New York: Crown Publishers, 1945,
pp. 631–694.

67 *Chafed Elbows*
Goosedown Productions, 1967.
Directed by Robert Downey.
Original screenplay by Robert Downey.
Chafed Elbows, by Robert Downey. New York: Lancer Books,
1967, 144 pp.

68 *Champion*
Stanley Kramer/United Artists, 1949.
Directed by Mark Robson.
Screenplay by Carl Foreman.
Based on the story by Ring Lardner.
The Moving Image, by Robert Gessner. New York: E. P.
Dutton & Co., 1968, pp. 57–58 (excerpt).

69 *Chance of a Lifetime*
Pilgrim Pictures, 1950.
Directed by Bernard Miles.
Original screenplay by Walter Greenwood and Bernard Miles.
The Cinema 1952, edited by Roger Manvell and R. K. Neilson
Baxter. Harmondsworth, Middlesex: Penguin Books, 1952,
pp. 12–18 (excerpt).

70 *The Chap from Broadway*
Produced under another title (short).
Directed by Eustace Hale Ball.
Original scenario by Eustace Hale Ball.

The Art of the Photoplay, by Eustace Hale Ball. New York:
G. W. Dillingham Company, 1913, pp. 103–115.

71 *The Chicken Inspector*
Vitagraph, 1914 (short).
Directed by Wallie Van and Wilfred North.
Original scenario by Roy L. McCardell.
Elbert Moore's Text Book on Writing the Photoplay. Chicago:
Elbert Moore, 1915, pp. 186–204.

72 *Un Chien Andalou (An Andalusian Dog)*
Luis Buñuel, 1928 (short).
Directed by Luis Buñuel.
Original scenario by Luis Buñuel and Salvador Dali.
Luis Buñuel, by Ado Kyrou. New York: Simon and Schuster,
1963, pp. 142–149.
L'Age d'Or and Un Chien Andalou, by Luis Buñuel. London:
Lorrimer Publishing, 1968, pp. 85–116. New York: Simon
and Schuster, 1968, pp. 85–116.

73 *Children of Paradise (Les Enfants du Paradis)*
S. N. Pathé Cinéma, 1945.
Directed by Marcel Carné.
Original screenplay by Jacques Prévert.
Les Enfants du Paradis, by Marcel Carné. London: Lorrimer
Publishing, 1968, 218 pp.
Children of Paradise, by Marcel Carné. New York: Simon and
Schuster, 1968, 218 pp.

74 *China Is Near (La Cina e Vicina)*
Vides Cinematografica S.A.S., 1967.
Directed by Marco Bellocchio.

Screenplay by Elda Tattoli and Marco Bellocchio.
Based on an original story by Marco Bellocchio.
China Is Near, by Marco Bellocchio. New York: The Orion
Press, 1969, 160 pp. London: Calder and Boyars, 1970,
160 pp.

75 *La Chinoise*
Anouchka-Athos-Parc-Simar, 1967.
Directed by Jean-Luc Godard.
Original screenplay by Jean-Luc Godard.
Jean-Luc Godard, by Jean Collet. New York: Crown Publishers,
1970, pp. 140-148 (excerpts).

76 *The Citadel*
Metro-Goldwyn-Mayer, 1938.
Directed by King Vidor.
Screenplay by Ian Dalrymple, Frank Wead and Elizabeth Hill.
Additional dialogue by Emlyn Williams.
Based on the novel by A. J. Cronin.
Foremost Films of 1938, by Frank Vreeland. New York and
Chicago: Pitman Publishing Corporation, 1939, pp. 147–163
(excerpts).

77 *Citizen Kane*
Mercury/RKO Radio, 1941.
Directed by Orson Welles.
Original screenplay by Herman J. Mankiewicz and Orson
Welles.
*Confrontation des Meilleurs Films de Tous les Temps
(Presentation of the Best Films of All Time)*. Brussels:
Belgian Film Library, 1958, pp. IX-1–IX-29 (excerpts).

The Cinema of Orson Welles, by Peter Cowie. London: A.
Zwemmer, 1965, pp. 39–48 (excerpts). New York: A. S.
Barnes & Co., 1965, pp. 39–48 (excerpts).
The Moving Image, by Robert Gessner. New York: E. P.
Dutton & Co., 1968, pp. 183–190 (excerpts).

78 *Coming Apart*
Kaleidoscope Films, 1969.
Directed by Milton Moses Ginsberg.
Original screenplay by Milton Moses Ginsberg.
Coming Apart, by Milton Moses Ginsberg. New York: Lancer
Books, 1969, 205 pp.

79 *Conquest of the Dark*
Associated British-Pathé, 19?? (documentary short).
Directed by Douglas Clarke.
How to Write Commentaries for Films, by Maurice Kirsch.
London and New York: Focal Press, 1956, pp. 69–78
(excerpt).

80 *Cosmopolitan*
Unproduced.
Screenplay by F. Scott Fitzgerald, based on his story "Babylon
Revisited".
The Moving Image, by Robert Gessner. New York: E. P.
Dutton & Co., 1968, pp. 243–247 (excerpts).

81 *Cyprus Is an Island*
Greenpark, 1946 (documentary short).
Directed by Ralph Keene.
Story and commentary by Laurie Lee.

We Made a Film in Cyprus, by Laurie Lee and Ralph Keene.
London: Longmans, Green and Co., 1947, pp. 79–92.

82 *David Copperfield*
Omnibus/Twentieth Century-Fox, 1970.
Directed by Delbert Mann.
Screenplay by Jack Pulman.
Based on the novel by Charles Dickens.
Copperfield '70, by George Curry. New York: Ballantine
Books, 1970, pp. 111–210.

83 *Death and Mathematics*
U. S. Office of War Information, 194? (documentary short).
Directed by Irving Lerner.
Script by Ben Maddow.
Hollywood Quraterly, I, No. 2 (January 1946), 173–181.

84 *Death Goes to School*
Independent Artists, 1953.
Directed by Stephen Clarkson.
Screenplay by Stephen Clarkson and Maisie Sharman.
Based on the novel *Death in Seven Hours* by Maisie Sharman.
How to Write Film Stories for Amateur Films, by Richard
Harrison. London and New York: Focal Press, 1954,
pp. 87–99 (excerpts, as "One Is Guilty").

85 *Descent to the Lower Depths*
Unproduced.
Scenario (unfinished) by Maxim Gorky, based on his play
The Lower Depths.
Films, I, No. 1 (November 1939), 40–50.
Cinemages, No. 9 (August 1, 1958), pp. 29–37.

86 *Destry Rides Again*
Universal, 1939.
Directed by George Marshall.
Screenplay by Felix Jackson, Gertrude Purcell and Henry Myers.
Based on an original story by Felix Jackson.
Suggested by the novel by Max Brand (pseud. of Frederick Faust).
The Best Pictures, 1939-1940, edited by Jerry Wald and Richard Macaulay. New York: Dodd, Mead & Company, 1940, pp. 289–330 (excerpts).

87 *The Devil's Disciple*
Unproduced.
Screenplay by Bernard Shaw, based on his play.
(Another version, scripted by John Dighton and Roland Kibbee, was filmed in 1959.)
The Serpent's Eye, by Donald P. Costello. Notre Dame: University of Notre Dame Press, 1965, pp. 163–164 (excerpts).

88 *The Dispossessed*
Unproduced.
Original screenplay by Errol John.
Force Majeure; The Dispossessed; Hasta Luego, by Errol John. London: Faber and Faber, 1967, pp. 77–143.

89 *The Doctor and the Devils*
Unproduced.
Screenplay by Dylan Thomas.
Based on the story by Donald Taylor.

The Doctor and the Devils, by Dylan Thomas. London: J. M.
Dent & Sons, 1953, 138 pp. New York: New Directions,
1953, 138 pp. New York: Time Incorporated, 1964, 177 pp.
The Doctor and the Devils and Other Scripts, by Dylan Thomas.
New York: New Directions, 1966, pp. 1–134.
Cinemages, No. 9 (August 1, 1958), pp. 71–80 (excerpts).

90   *Dr. Ehrlich's Magic Bullet*
Warner Bros., 1940.
Directed by William Dieterle.
Original screenplay by John Huston, Heinz Herald and
Norman Burnside.
Based on an idea by Norman Burnside.
The Best Pictures, 1939-1940, edited by Jerry Wald and Richard
Macaulay. New York: Dodd, Mead & Company, 1940,
pp. 241–288 (excerpts).

91   *Doctor Zhivago*
Sostar/Metro-Goldwyn-Mayer, 1965.
Directed by David Lean.
Screenplay by Robert Bolt.
Based on the novel by Boris Pasternak.
Doctor Zhivago, by Robert Bolt. New York: Random House,
1965, 224 pp.

92   *La Dolce Vita*
Riama Film, 1960.
Directed by Federico Fellini.
Screenplay by Federico Fellini, Tullio Pinelli, Ennio Flaiano
and Brunello Rondi.
Based on an original story by Federico Fellini, Tullio Pinelli
and Ennio Flaiano.

La Dolce Vita, by Federico Fellini. New York: Ballantine
   Books, 1961, 274 pp.
Federico Fellini, by Gilbert Salachas. New York: Crown
   Publishers, 1969, pp. 148–155 (excerpts).

93   *Don't Look Back*
Leacock Pennebaker, 1967 (documentary).
Bob Dylan: Don't Look Back, by D. A. Pennebaker. New York:
   Ballantine Books, 1968, 152 pp.

94   *Double Indemnity*
Paramount, 1944.
Directed by Billy Wilder.
Screenplay by Billy Wilder and Raymond Chandler.
Based on the novel by James M. Cain.
Best Film Plays—1945, edited by John Gassner and Dudley
   Nichols. New York: Crown Publishers, 1946, pp. 115–174.

95   *Dragon Seed*
Metro-Goldwyn-Mayer, 1944.
Directed by Jack Conway and Harold S. Bucquet.
Screenplay by Marguerite Roberts and Jane Murfin.
Based on the novel by Pearl S. Buck.
Best Film Plays of 1943-1944, edited by John Gassner and
   Dudley Nichols. New York: Crown Publishers, 1945,
   pp. 357–449.

96   *The Dynasts*
Unproduced.
Screenplay by Dallas Bower.
Based on the play by Thomas Hardy.

Plan for Cinema, by Dallas Bower. London: J. M. Dent & Sons, 1936, pp. 77–98 (excerpts).

97   *Eastern Valley*
Strand, 1937 (documentary short).
Directed by Donald Alexander.
Script by Donald Alexander and Paul Rotha.
One-Reel Scenarios for Amateur Movie-Makers, edited by
   Margaret Mayorga. New York: Samuel French, 1938,
   pp. 183–194.

98   *Easy Rider*
Pando-Raybert/Columbia, 1969.
Directed by Dennis Hopper.
Original screenplay by Peter Fonda, Dennis Hopper and
   Terry Southern.
Easy Rider, by Peter Fonda, Dennis Hopper and Terry Southern.
   New York: New American Library (Signet Books), 1969,
   191 pp.

99   *L'Eclisse (The Eclipse)*
Interopa Film–Cineriz–Paris Film, 1962.
Directed by Michelangelo Antonioni.
Screenplay by Michelangelo Antonioni, Tonino Guerra, Elio
   Bartolini and Ottiero Ottieri.
Based on an original story by Michelangelo Antonioni and
   Tonino Guerra.
Screenplays of Michelangelo Antonioni. New York: The Orion
   Press, 1963, pp. 277–361.

100   8½ (*Otto e Mezzo*)
Cineriz, 1963.
Directed by Federico Fellini.
Screenplay by Federico Fellini, Tullio Pinelli, Ennio Flaiano
and Brunello Rondi.
Based on an original story by Federico Fellini and Ennio
Flaiano.
Federico Fellini, by Gilbert Salachas. New York: Crown
Publishers, 1969, pp. 156–163 (excerpts).

101   *8 x 8*
Hans Richter, 1955.
Directed by Hans Richter.
Original screenplay by Hans Richter.
Film Culture, I, No. 5–6 (Winter 1955), 17–19 (excerpt).

102   *Encore*
Two Cities, 1951.
Part I: "The Ant and the Grasshopper." Directed by Pat
Jackson. Screenplay by T. E. B. Clarke.
Part II: "Winter Cruise." Directed by Anthony Pelissier.
Screenplay by Arthur MacRae.
Part III: "Gigolo and Gigolette." Directed by Harold French.
Screenplay by Eric Ambler.
Based on the stories by W. Somerset Maugham.
Encore, by W. Somerset Maugham. London: William
Heinemann, 1952, 165 pp. Garden City: Doubleday &
Company, 1952, 156 pp.

103   *The End of the Affair*
Coronado/Columbia, 1954.
Directed by Edward Dmytryk.

Screenplay by Lenore Coffee.
Based on the novel by Graham Greene.
The Moving Image, by Robert Gessner. New York: E. P.
Dutton & Co., 1968, pp. 279–281 (excerpt).

104   *An Enemy of the People*
Unproduced.
Screenplay by Mo Wax.
Based on the play by Henrik Ibsen.
Film Writing Forms, edited by Lewis Jacobs. New York:
Gotham Book Mart, 1934, pp. 45–58.

105   *The Exterminating Angel* (*El Angel Exterminador*)
Gustavo Alatriste, 1962.
Directed by Luis Buñuel.
Screenplay by Luis Buñuel.
Based on a story by Luis Buñuel and Luis Alcoriza, suggested
by an unpublished play by José Bergamin.
Three Screen Plays, by Luis Buñuel. New York: The Orion
Press, 1969, pp. 111–195.

106   *A Face in the Crowd*
Newtown/Warner Bros., 1957.
Directed by Elia Kazan.
Screenplay by Budd Schulberg, based on his story "Your
Arkansas Traveler."
A Face in the Crowd, by Budd Schulberg. New York: Random
House, 1957, 172 pp. New York: Bantam Books, 1957,
155 pp.

107 *Fahrenheit 451*
Vineyard/Universal, 1966.
Directed by François Truffaut.
Screenplay by François Truffaut and Jean-Louis Richard.
Based on the novel by Ray Bradbury.
The Moving Image, by Robert Gessner. New York: E. P.
Dutton & Co., 1968, pp. 338–339, 374–376 (excerpts).

108 *The Fallen Idol*
London Films, 1948.
Directed by Carol Reed.
Screenplay by Graham Greene.
Additional dialogue by Lesley Storm and William Templeton.
Based on the story "The Basement Room" by Graham Greene.
Teaching About the Film, by J. M. L. Peters. New York:
International Documents Service (Columbia University
Press), 1961, pp. 25–27 (excerpt).

109 *Fellini Satyricon*
Produzioni Europee Associate/United Artists, 1969.
Directed by Federico Fellini.
Screenplay by Federico Fellini and Bernardino Zapponi, with
the collaboration of Brunello Rondi.
Based on *Satyricon* by Petronius, *The Golden Ass* by Apuleius,
Metamorphoses by Ovid, *Satires* by Horace, and *Lives of
the Caesars* by Suetonius.
Fellini's Satyricon, by Federico Fellini. New York: Ballantine
Books, 1970, 280 pp.

110 *Une Femme Est une Femme* (*A Woman Is a Woman*)
Rome-Paris Films, 1961.
Directed by Jean-Luc Godard.

Screenplay by Jean-Luc Godard.

Based on an idea by Geneviève Cluny.

Jean-Luc Godard, by Jean Collet. New York: Crown Publishers, 1970, pp. 114–126 (excerpts).

111 *Ferghana Canal*
Unproduced.

Original screenplay by Sergei M. Eisenstein and Pyotr Pavlenko.

The Film Sense, by Sergei M. Eisenstein. New York: Harcourt, Brace and Company, 1942, pp. 256–268 (excerpt).

112 *The Fight for Life*
United States Film Service, 1940.

Directed by Pare Lorentz.

Screenplay by Pare Lorentz.

Based on the book by Paul de Kruif.

Twenty Best Film Plays, edited by John Gassner and Dudley Nichols. New York: Crown Publishers, 1943, pp. 1081–1111.

113 *Film*
Evergreen Theatre, 1965 (short).

Directed by Alan Schneider.

Original screenplay by Samuel Beckett.

Film, by Samuel Beckett. New York: Grove Press, 1969, 95 pp.

114 *The Fire Jugglers*
Selig Polyscope, 1914 (short).

Original scenario by William E. Wing.

How to Write a Photoplay, by Arthur Winfield Thomas. Chicago: Photoplaywrights Association of America, 1914, pp. 91–98.

115   *The Firemen's Social*
Biograph, 1914 (split-reel).
How to Write a Photoplay, by Arthur Winfield Thomas.
Chicago: Photoplaywrights Association of America, 1914,
pp. 128–133.

116   *Flower of the North*
Vitagraph, 1921.
Directed by David Smith.
Scenario by Bradley J. Smollen.
Based on the novel by James Oliver Curwood.
Screen Acting, by Inez and Helen Klumph. New York: Falk
Publishing Co., 1922, pp. 155–161 (excerpt).

117   *Fogg's Millions*
Vitagraph, 1914 (short).
Directed by Van Dyke Brooke.
Original scenario by Elizabeth R. Carpenter.
How to Write a Photoplay, by Arthur Winfield Thomas.
Chicago: Photoplaywrights Association of America, 1914,
pp. 176–189.

118   *Force Majeure*
Unproduced.
Original screenplay by Errol John.
Force Majeure; The Dispossessed; Hasta Luego, by Errol John.
London: Faber and Faber, 1967, pp. 11–73.

119   *The Forgotten Village*
Herbert Kline, 1941 (documentary)

Directed by Herbert Kline.
Story and script by John Steinbeck.
The Forgotten Village, by John Steinbeck. New York: The
Viking Press, 1941, 143 pp.

120   *The 400 Blows (Les Quatre Cents Coups)*
S.E.D.I.F.-Les Films du Carrosse, 1959.
Directed by François Truffaut.
Screenplay by Marcel Moussy.
Based on an original story by François Truffaut.
The 400 Blows, by François Truffaut. New York: Grove Press,
1969, 255 pp.

121   *Friend John*
Lubin, 1913 (short).
Directed by Arthur Johnson.
Original scenario by Lawrence S. McCloskey.
The Technique of the Photoplay, by Epes Winthrop Sargent.
New York: The Moving Picture World, 1913 (Second
edition), pp. 165–173.

122   *From Here to Eternity*
Columbia, 1953.
Directed by Fred Zinnemann.
Screenplay by Daniel Taradash.
Based on the novel by James Jones.
The Moving Image, by Robert Gessner. New York: E. P.
Dutton & Co., 1968, pp. 32–34, 299–301 (excerpts).

123   *Fury*
Metro-Goldwyn-Mayer, 1936.
Directed by Fritz Lang.

Screenplay by Bartlett Cormack and Fritz Lang.
Based on an original story by Norman Krasna.
Twenty Best Film Plays, edited by John Gassner and Dudley
Nichols. New York: Crown Publishers, 1943, pp. 521–582.

124   *G. I. Joe*
Lester Cowan/United Artists, 1945.
Directed by William A. Wellman.
Screenplay by Leopold Atlas, Guy Endore and Philip Stevenson.
Based on the book *Here Is Your War* by Ernie Pyle.
Best Film Plays—1945, edited by John Gassner and Dudley
Nichols. New York: Crown Publishers, 1946, pp. 381–425.
Theatre Arts, XXIX, No. 9 (September 1945), 514–520
(excerpt).

125   *Gaslight*
British National, 1940.
Directed by Thorold Dickinson.
Screenplay by A. R. Rawlinson and Bridget Boland.
Based on the play *Angel Street* by Patrick Hamilton.
The Art of the Film, by Ernest Lindgren. London: George
Allen and Unwin, 1948, pp. 185-193 (excerpt).

126   *A Gay Old Dog*
Pathé, 1919.
Directed by Hobart Henley.
Scenario by Mrs. Sidney Drew.
Based on the story "The Gay Old Dog" by Edna Ferber.
The Feature Photoplay, by Henry Albert Phillips. Springfield:
The Home Correspondence School, 1921, pp. 280–284
(excerpt).

36

127 *The Ghost Goes West*
London Films, 1936.
Directed by René Clair.
Screenplay by Robert E. Sherwood.
Adaptation by Geoffrey Kerr.
Based on the story "Sir Tristram Goes West" by Eric Keown.
Successful Film Writing, by Seton Margrave. London: Methuen
& Co., 1936, pp. 69–216.

128 *Giro di Roma*
B. B. C., 1961 (documentary).
Written and directed by Edouard de Laurot.
Film Culture, No. 22–23 (Summer 1961), pp. 171–195
(excerpts).

129 *The Goddess*
Carnegie/Columbia, 1958.
Directed by John Cromwell.
Original screenplay by Paddy Chayefsky.
The Goddess, by Paddy Chayefsky. New York: Simon and
Schuster, 1958, 167 pp.
Elements of Film, by Lee R. Bobker. New York: Harcourt,
Brace & World, 1969, pp. 23–28 (excerpt).

130 *Going My Way*
Paramount, 1944.
Directed by Leo McCarey.
Screenplay by Frank Butler and Frank Cavett.
Based on an original story by Leo McCarey.
Best Film Plays of 1943-1944, edited by John Gassner and
Dudley Nichols. New York: Crown Publishers, 1945,
pp. 149–222.

131 *The Gold Rush*
Charles Chaplin/United Artists, 1925.
Directed by Charles Chaplin.
Original scenario by Charles Chaplin.
Cinema, IV, No. 2 (Summer 1968), 17–44 (script compiled
   from the film by Timothy J. Lyons).

132 *The Golem* (*Der Golem*)
Ufa, 1920.
Directed by Paul Wegener.
Scenario by Henrik Galeen.
Adapted from Gustav Meyrink.
Films of Tyranny, by Richard B. Byrne. Madison, Wisconsin:
   College Printing & Typing Co., 1966, pp. 43–96 (shot
   analysis).

133 *The Good Earth*
Metro-Goldwyn-Mayer, 1937.
Directed by Sidney Franklin.
Screenplay by Talbot Jennings, Tess Slesinger and Claudine
   West.
(Contributor to screenplay construction: Frances Marion.
   Contributors to dialogue: Marc Connelly and Jules
   Furthman.)
Based on the novel by Pearl S. Buck.
Twenty Best Film Plays, edited by John Gassner and Dudley
   Nichols. New York: Crown Publishers, 1943, pp. 875–950.
Great Film Plays, edited by John Gassner and Dudley Nichols.
   New York: Crown Publishers, 1959, pp. 171–246.

134 *Goodbye, Mr. Chips*
Metro-Goldwyn-Mayer, 1939.
Directed by Sam Wood.
Screenplay by R. C. Sherriff, Claudine West and Eric Maschwitz.
Based on the novel by James Hilton.
The Best Pictures, 1939-1940, edited by Jerry Wald and Richard
  Macaulay. New York: Dodd, Mead & Company, 1940,
  pp. 31–78 (excerpts).

135 *Grand Illusion* (*La Grande Illusion*)
Réalisations d'Art Cinématographique, 1937.
Directed by Jean Renoir.
Original screenplay by Charles Spaak and Jean Renoir.
La Grande Illusion, by Jean Renoir. London: Lorrimer
  Publishing, 1968, 104 pp.
Grand Illusion, by Jean Renoir. New York: Simon and Schuster,
  1968, 104 pp.

136 *Les Grandes Manoeuvres* (*The Grand Maneuver*)
Filmsonor, 1955.
Directed by René Clair.
Screenplay by René Clair, assisted by Jérôme Géronimi and
  Jean Marsan.
Based on a story by Georges Courteline (pseud. of Georges
  Moineaux).
Four Screenplays, by René Clair. New York: The Orion Press,
  1970, pp. 321–435.

137 *The Grapes of Wrath*
Twentieth Century-Fox, 1940.
Directed by John Ford.

Screenplay by Nunnally Johnson.
Based on the novel by John Steinbeck.
Twenty Best Film Plays, edited by John Gassner and Dudley
Nichols. New York: Crown Publishers, 1943, pp. 333–377.

138 *Great Expectations*
Universal, 1934.
Directed by Stuart Walker.
Screenplay by Gladys Unger.
Based on the novel by Charles Dickens.
Money for Film Stories, by Norman Lee. London: Sir Isaac
Pitman & Sons, 1937, p. 120 (excerpt).
The Moving Image, by Robert Gessner. New York: E. P.
Dutton & Co., 1968, pp. 289–290, 296–297 (excerpts).

139 *Great Expectations*
Cineguild, 1946.
Directed by David Lean.
Screenplay by David Lean, Ronald Neame and Anthony
Havelock-Allan.
Additional dialogue by Cecil McGivern and Kay Walsh.
Based on the novel by Charles Dickens.
The Cinema 1952, edited by Roger Manvell and R. K. Neilson
Baxter. Harmondsworth, Middlesex: Penguin Books,
1952, pp. 20–29 (excerpt).
The Moving Image, by Robert Gessner. New York: E. P.
Dutton & Co., 1968, pp. 291–292, 297–298 (excerpts).

140 *The Great Game*
Essanay, 1913 (short).
Original scenario by Maibelle Heikes Justice.

The Motion Picture Story, by William Lord Wright. Chicago: Cloud Publishing Company, 1914, pp. 92–113.

141 *The Great Moment*
Famous Players-Lasky/Paramount, 1921.
Directed by Sam Wood.
Scenario by Monte M. Katterjohn.
Based on an original story by Elinor Glyn.
The Elinor Glyn System of Writing, by Elinor Glyn. Auburn, N. Y.: The Authors' Press, 1922, Vol. 4, pp. 409–500.

142 *The Great Train Robbery*
Edison, 1903 (short).
Directed by Edwin S. Porter.
Original scenario by Edwin S. Porter.
First published in the Edison Catalogue of 1904.
The Rise of the American Film, by Lewis Jacobs. New York: Harcourt, Brace and Company, 1939, pp. 43–46.
The Emergence of Film Art, by Lewis Jacobs. New York: Hopkinson and Blake, 1969, pp. 28–30.

143 *Greed*
Metro-Goldwyn, 1924.
Directed by Erich von Stroheim.
Scenario by Erich von Stroheim.
Based on the novel *McTeague* by Frank Norris.
Greed, by Erich von Stroheim. Brussels: Belgian Film Library, 1958, 274 pp.
The Moving Image, by Robert Gessner. New York: E. P. Dutton & Co., 1968, pp. 213–221, 316–317, 323 (excerpts).

144   *Il Grido* (*The Outcry*)
S.P.A. Cinematografica, 1957.
Directed by Michelangelo Antonioni.
Screenplay by Michelangelo Antonioni, Elio Bartolini and
   Ennio De Concini.
Based on an original story by Michelangelo Antonioni.
Screenplays of Michelangelo Antonioni. New York: The
   Orion Press, 1963, pp. 1–92.
Michelangelo Antonioni, by Pierre Leprohon. New York:
   Simon and Schuster, 1963, pp. 131–140 (excerpt).

145   *La Guerre Est Finie* (*The War Is Over*)
Sofracima–Europa-Film, 1966.
Directed by Alain Resnais.
Original screenplay by Jorge Semprun.
La Guerre Est Finie, by Jorge Semprun. New York: Grove
   Press, 1967, 192 pp.

146   *Hail the Conquering Hero*
Paramount, 1944.
Directed by Preston Sturges.
Original screenplay by Preston Sturges.
Best Film Plays of 1943–1944, edited by John Gassner and
   Dudley Nichols. New York: Crown Publishers, 1945,
   pp. 561–630.

147   *Hail the Woman*
Thomas H. Ince/First National, 1921.
Directed by John Griffith Wray.
Original scenario by C. Gardner Sullivan.

Synopsis and Continuity of Hail the Woman, by C. Gardner
  Sullivan. New York: Palmer Photoplay Corp., 1921, 125 pp.
Palmer Handbook of Scenario Construction, by Frederick
  Palmer. N. p., n.d., Vol. 2, pp. 500–531 (excerpts).

148 *Hamlet*
Two Cities, 1948.
Directed by Laurence Olivier.
Screenplay adapted by Alan Dent.
From the play by William Shakespeare.
Hollywood Quarterly, III, No. 3 (Spring 1948), 293–300
  (excerpt).
The Moving Image, by Robert Gessner. New York: E. P.
  Dutton & Co., 1968, pp. 132–136, 239–240 (excerpts).

149 *Harlot*
Andy Warhol, 1965.
Directed by Andy Warhol.
Original screenplay by Ronald Tavel, Harry Fainlight and
  Billy Linich.
Film Culture, No. 40 (Spring 1966), pp. 57–65.

150 *Hasta Luego*
Unproduced.
Original screenplay by Errol John.
Force Majeure; The Dispossessed; Hasta Luego, by Errol John.
  London: Faber and Faber, 1967, pp. 147–194.

151 *The Heir of the Ages*
Pallas/Paramount, 1917.
Directed by E. J. Le Saint.
Original scenario by William Addison Lathrop.

Little Stories from the Screen, by William Addison Lathrop.
New York: Britton Publishing Company, 1917, pp. 279–324.

152   *The Heiress*
Paramount, 1949.
Directed by William Wyler.
Screenplay by Ruth and Augustus Goetz, based on their play,
and on the novel *Washington Square* by Henry James.
The Moving Image, by Robert Gessner. New York: E. P.
Dutton & Co., 1968, pp. 94–98, 307–309 (excerpts).

153   *Henry V*
Two Cities, 1944.
Directed by Laurence Olivier.
Screenplay adapted by Laurence Olivier, Alan Dent and
Reginald Beck.
From the play by William Shakespeare.
The Moving Image, by Robert Gessner. New York: E. P.
Dutton & Co., 1968, pp. 283–285 (excerpts).

154   *Here Comes Mr. Jordan*
Columbia, 1941.
Directed by Alexander Hall.
Screenplay by Sidney Buchman and Seton I. Miller.
Based on the play *Heaven Can Wait* by Harry Segall.
Twenty Best Film Plays, edited by John Gassner and Dudley
Nichols. New York: Crown Publishers, 1943, pp. 181–231.

155   *The Hill*
Unproduced.
Original screenplay by Howard Fast.

The Hill, by Howard Fast. Garden City: Doubleday &
Company, 1964, 123 pp.

156   *Hiroshima Mon Amour*
Argos-Daiei-Como-Pathé, 1959.
Directed by Alain Resnais.
Original screenplay by Marguerite Duras.
Hiroshima Mon Amour, by Marguerite Duras. New York:
Grove Press, 1961, 112 pp.
Hiroshima Mon Amour; Une Aussi Longue Absence, by
Marguerite Duras. London: Calder and Boyars, 1966,
pp. 17–79.
Elements of Film, by Lee R. Bobker. New York: Harcourt,
Brace & World, 1969, pp. 14–19, 47–48 (excerpts).

157   *His Old-Fashioned Mother*
Produced under another title (short).
Directed by Eustace Hale Ball.
Original scenario by Eustace Hale Ball.
Photoplay Scenarios, by Eustace Hale Ball. New York: Hearst's
International Library Co., 1915, pp. 142–160.
Cinema Plays, by Eustace Hale Ball. London: Stanley Paul &
Co., 1917, pp. 108–123.

158   *His Suicide*
Lubin, 1914 (short).
Directed by J. T. Hevener.
Original scenario by Epes Winthrop Sargent.
How to Write for the "Movies," by Louella O. Parsons.
Chicago: A. C. McClurg & Co., 1917, pp. 122–126.

159   *An Honest Man* (*Un Honnête Homme*)
S.O.F.A.C.
Directed by Ado Kyrou.
Original screenplay by Ado Kyrou.
An Honest Man, by Ado Kyrou. London: Rodney Books, 1964,
[40 pp.]

160   *The House*
Unproduced.
Original screenplay by James Agee.
New Letters in America, edited by Horace Gregory. New York:
W .W. Norton & Company, 1937, pp. 37–55.
Cinemages, No. 9 (August 1, 1958), pp. 5–18.
The Collected Short Prose of James Agee. Boston: Houghton
Mifflin Company, 1968, pp. 151–173.

161   *House of Incest*
Unproduced.
Original scenario by Anaïs Nin.
Cinemages, No. 9 (August 1, 1958), pp. 38–39.

162   *The Householder*
Merchant-Ivory, 1963.
Directed by James Ivory.
Screenplay by Ruth Prawer Jhabvala, based on her novel.
The Householder, by R. Prawer Jhabvala. Delhi: Ramlochan
Books, n.d., 168 pp.

163   *How Green Was My Valley*
Twentieth Century-Fox, 1941.
Directed by John Ford.

Screenplay by Philip Dunne.
Based on the novel by Richard Llewellyn.
Twenty Best Film Plays, edited by John Gassner and Dudley
Nichols. New York: Crown Publishers, 1943, pp. 379–431.

164   *The Human Comedy*
Metro-Goldwyn-Mayer, 1943.
Directed by Clarence Brown.
Screenplay by Howard Estabrook.
Based on the novel by William Saroyan.
Drama in Our Time, by M. M. Nagelberg. New York:
Harcourt, Brace and Company, 1948, pp. 418–437 (excerpts).

165   *I Am Curious (Blue)* (*Jag Ar Nyfiken—Blaa*)
Sandrews, 1968.
Directed by Vilgot Sjöman.
Original screenplay by Vilgot Sjöman.
I Am Curious (Blue), by Vilgot Sjöman. New York: Grove
Press, 1970, 219 pp.

166   *I Am Curious (Yellow)* (*Jag Ar Nyfiken—Gul*)
Sandrews, 1967.
Directed by Vilgot Sjöman.
Original screenplay by Vilgot Sjöman.
I Am Curious (Yellow), by Vilgot Sjöman. New York: Grove
Press, 1968, 254 pp.

167   *If. . . .*
Memorial Enterprises/Paramount, 1969.
Directed by Lindsay Anderson.

Screenplay by David Sherwin.

Based on an original script, "Crusaders," by David Sherwin and John Howlett.

If. . . ., by Lindsay Anderson and David Sherwin. London: Lorrimer Publishing, 1969, 167 pp. New York: Simon and Schuster, 1970, 167 pp.

168 *If I Were Young Again*
Selig Polyscope, 1914 (short).
Directed by F. J. Grandon.
Original scenario by Gilson Willets.

How to Write Photoplays, by Clarence J. Caine. Philadelphia: David McKay, 1915, pp. 245-255. New York: Street & Smith, 1915, pp. 245–255.

169 *Ikiru (To Live)*
Toho, 1952.
Directed by Akira Kurosawa.
Original screenplay by Shinobu Hashimoto, Hideo Oguni and Akira Kurosawa.

Ikiru, by Akira Kurosawa. London: Lorrimer Publishing, 1968, 84 pp. New York: Simon and Schuster, 1968, 84 pp.

170 *I'm an Explosive!*
George Smith/Fox Films, 1933.
Directed by Adrian Brunel.
Screenplay by Adrian Brunel.
Based on the novel *High Explosive* by Gordon Phillips.

Filmcraft, by Adrian Brunel. London: George Newnes, 1936, pp. 118–140 (excerpts).

171   *The Importance of Being Earnest*
British Film Makers, 1952.
Directed by Anthony Asquith.
Screenplay by Anthony Asquith.
Based on the play by Oscar Wilde.
The Moving Image, by Robert Gessner. New York: E. P. Dutton
& Co., 1968, pp. 359–360 (excerpt).

172   *In Old Chicago*
Twentieth Century-Fox, 1938.
Directed by Henry King.
Screenplay by Lamar Trotti and Sonya Levien.
(Contributor to treatment: Richard Collins.)
Based on an original story, "We, the O'Learys," by Niven Busch.
In Old Chicago, by Lamar Trotti and Sonya Levien. Beverly
Hills: Twentieth Century-Fox Film Corp., 1937, 263 pp.
Foremost Films of 1938, by Frank Vreeland. New York and
Chicago: Pitman Publishing Corporation, 1939, pp. 79–96
(excerpts).

173   *In the Mesh* (*L'Engrenage*)
Unproduced.
Original screenplay by Jean-Paul Sartre.
In the Mesh, by Jean-Paul Sartre. London: Andrew Dakers
Limited, 1954, 128 pp.

174   *In the Old Attic*
Vitagraph, 1913 (short).
Directed by Frederick Tomson.
Original scenario by Catherine Carr.
The Art of Photoplay Writing, by Catherine Carr. New York:
The Hannis Jordan Company, 1914, pp. 54–75.

175 *The Informer*
RKO Radio, 1935.
Directed by John Ford.
Screenplay by Dudley Nichols.
Based on the novel by Liam O'Flaherty.

Modern British Dramas, edited by Harlan Hatcher. New York:
Harcourt, Brace and Company, 1941, pp. 301–367.
Modern Dramas, edited by Harlan Hatcher. New York:
Harcourt, Brace and Company, 1944, pp. 199–265.
Theatre Arts, XXXV, No. 8 (August 1951), 60–82.
The Moving Image, by Robert Gessner. New York: E. P. Dutton
& Co., 1968, pp. 163–170 (excerpts).

176 *Intolerance*
Wark, 1916.
Directed by D. W. Griffith.
Original scenario by D. W. Griffith.
Titles by Anita Loos.

*Intolerance. The Film by David Wark Griffith. Shot-by-Shot
Analysis* by Theodore Huff. New York: The Museum of
Modern Art, 1966, 155 pp.
The Rise of the American Film, by Lewis Jacobs. New York:
Harcourt, Brace and Company, 1939, pp. 193–197 (excerpt).

177 *Irma La Douce*
Mirisch-Phalanx/United Artists, 1963.
Directed by Billy Wilder.
Screenplay by Billy Wilder and I. A. L. Diamond.
Based on the play by Alexandre Breffort.

Irma La Douce, by Billy Wilder and I. A. L. Diamond.
New York: Tower Publications, 1963, 128 pp.

178   It *Always Rains on Sunday*
Ealing Studios, 1947.
Directed by Robert Hamer.
Screenplay by Angus MacPhail, Robert Hamer and
   Henry Cornelius.
Based on the novel by Arthur J. La Bern.
A Film in the Making, by John W. Collier. London: World
   Film Publications, 1947, pp. 14–16, 59 (excerpts).

179   *It Happened One Night*
Columbia, 1934.
Directed by Frank Capra.
Screenplay by Robert Riskin.
Based on the story "Night Bus" by Samuel Hopkins Adams.
Four-Star Scripts, edited by Lorraine Noble. Garden City:
   Doubleday, Doran & Company, 1936, pp. 124–212.
Twenty Best Film Plays, edited by John Gassner and Dudley
   Nichols. New York: Crown Publishers, 1943, pp. 1–59.
Great Film Plays, edited by John Gassner and Dudley Nichols.
   New York: Crown Publishers, 1959, p. 1–59.

180   *Ivan the Terrible*
Alma-Ata, 1944 (Part I); Mosfilm, 1946 (Part II).
Directed by Sergei M. Eisenstein.
Original screenplay by Sergei M. Eisenstein.
Ivan the Terrible, by Sergei M. Eisenstein. New York:
   Simon and Schuster, 1962, 319 pp.
The Moving Image, by Robert Gessner. New York: E. P. Dutton
   & Co., 1968, pp. 195–199 (excerpts).

181 *Jan Huss*
Czechoslovakia, 1957.
Directed by Otakar Vávra.
Original screenplay by Miloš V. Kratochvíl and Otakar Vávra,
  with motifs from Alois Jirásek.
John Huss, by M. V. Kratochvíl and O. Vávra. Prague:
  Artia, 1957, 174 pp.

182 *Jesus of Nazareth*
Unproduced.
Original screenplay by Carl Th. Dreyer.
Carl Th. Dreyer, edited by Søren Dyssegaard. Copenhagen:
  Ministry of Foreign Affairs, 1969, pp. 20–31 (excerpts).

183 *Jew Süss* (U. S. title: *Power*)
Gaumont British, 1934.
Directed by Lothar Mendes.
Screenplay by A. R. Rawlinson.
Adaptation by Dorothy Farnum.
Based on the novel by Lion Feuchtwanger.
Jew Süss, edited by Ernest Betts. London: Methuen & Co.,
  1935, 174 pp.

184 *Joan of Arc*
Sierra/RKO Radio, 1948.
Directed by Victor Fleming.
Screenplay by Maxwell Anderson and Andrew Solt.
Based on the play *Joan of Lorraine* by Maxwell Anderson.
Joan of Arc, by Maxwell Anderson and Andrew Solt. New York:
  William Sloane Associates, 1948, 172 pp. (excerpts).

185　*The Job* (*Il Lavoro*) (Part II of *Boccaccio '70*)
Concordia Compagnia Cinematografica-Cineriz-Francinex-
　Gray Film, 1961.
Directed by Luchino Visconti.
Screenplay by Suso Cecchi d'Amico and Luchino Visconti.
Based on the story "Au Bord du Lit" by Guy de Maupassant.
Three Screenplays, by Luchino Visconti. New York: The Orion
　Press, 1970, pp. 273–313.

186　*The Jolly Old Patriots*
Produced under another title (short).
Directed by Eustace Hale Ball.
Original scenario by Eustace Hale Ball.
Photoplay Scenarios, by Eustace Hale Ball. New York: Hearst's
　International Library Co., 1915, pp. 105–130.
Cinema Plays, by Eustace Hale Ball. London: Stanley Paul
　& Co., 1917, pp. 78–99.

187　*Juarez*
Warner Bros., 1939.
Directed by William Dieterle.
Screenplay by John Huston, Wolfgang Reinhardt and
　Aeneas MacKenzie.
Based on the play *Juarez and Maximilian* by Franz Werfel,
　and the novel *The Phantom Crown* by Bertita Harding.
Twenty Best Film Plays, edited by John Gassner and Dudley
　Nichols. New York: Crown Publishers, 1943, pp. 705–769.

188　*Judgment at Nuremberg*
Stanley Kramer/United Artists, 1961.
Directed by Stanley Kramer.
Screenplay by Abby Mann, based on his teleplay.

Judgment at Nuremberg, by Abby Mann. London: Cassell, 1961, 182 pp.

189 *Judgment of the Storm*
Palmer Photoplay Corp./F.B.O., 1923.
Directed by Del Andrews.
Original scenario by Ethel Styles Middleton.
Reference Scenarios. Hollywood: Palmer Institute of Authorship, 1924, pp. 1–294.

190 *Jules and Jim (Jules et Jim)*
Carrosse Films-S.E.D.I.F., 1962.
Directed by François Truffaut.
Screenplay by François Truffaut and Jean Gruault.
Based on the novel by Henri-Pierre Roche.
Jules and Jim, by François Truffaut. London: Lorrimer Publishing, 1968, 100 pp. New York: Simon and Schuster, 1968, 100 pp.

191 *Juliet of the Spirits (Giulietta degli Spiriti)*
Federiz, 1965.
Directed by Federico Fellini.
Screenplay by Federico Fellini, Tullio Pinelli, Ennio Flaiano and Brunello Rondi.
Based on an original story by Federico Fellini and Tullio Pinelli.
Juliet of the Spirits, by Federico Fellini. New York: Orion Press, 1965, 181 pp. New York: Ballantine Books, 1966, 318 pp.

192 *Julius Caesar*
Metro-Goldwyn-Mayer, 1953.
Directed by Joseph L. Mankiewicz.

Screenplay adapted by Joseph L. Mankiewicz.
From the play by William Shakespeare.
The Quarterly of Film, Radio, and Television, VIII, No. 2
(Winter 1953), 109–124 (excerpts).

193 *Just a Song at Twilight*
Dixie Film Co., 1922.
Directed by Carlton King.
Original scenario by Henry Albert Phillips.
The Feature Photoplay, by Henry Albert Phillips. Springfield:
The Home Correspondence School, 1921, pp. 274–277
(excerpts).

194 *Kind Hearts and Coronets*
Ealing Studios, 1949.
Directed by Robert Hamer.
Screenplay by Robert Hamer and John Dighton.
Based on the novel *Israel Rank* by Roy Horniman.
The Cinema 1952, edited by Roger Manvell and R. K. Neilson
Baxter. Harmondsworth, Middlesex: Penguin Books,
1952, pp. 54–66 (excerpt).

195 *The King Who Was a King*
Unproduced.
Original screenplay by H. G. Wells.
The King Who Was a King, by H. G. Wells. London: Ernest
Benn, 1929, 254 pp. Garden City: Doubleday, Doran &
Company, 1929, 272 pp.

196 *The Kingdom of the Earth* (*Le Royaume de la Terre*)
Unproduced.
Original screenplay by Abel Gance and Nelly Kaplan.

Film Culture, III, No. 5 (December 1957), 10–13; IV, No. 1
(January 1958), 14–16 (excerpts).

197   *A Kiss for Cinderella*
Famous Players-Lasky/Paramount, 1926.
Directed by Herbert Brenon.
Scenario by Willis Goldbeck and Townsend Martin.
Based on the play by James M. Barrie.
Motion Picture Continuities, edited by Frances Taylor Patterson.
   New York: Columbia University Press, 1929, pp. 1–87.

198   *Lady for a Day*
Columbia, 1933.
Directed by Frank Capra.
Screenplay by Robert Riskin.
Based on the story "Madame La Gimp" by Damon Runyon.
Four-Star Scripts, edited by Lorraine Noble. Garden City:
   Doubleday, Doran & Company, 1936, pp. 24–123.

199   *The Ladykillers*
Ealing Studios, 1956.
Directed by Alexander Mackendrick.
Original screenplay by William Rose.
The Living Screen, by Roger Manvell. London: George G. Harrap
   & Co., 1961, pp. 167–172 (excerpt).

200   *The Last Command*
Paramount, 1928.
Directed by Josef von Sternberg.
Scenario by John F. Goodrich.
Titles by Herman J. Mankiewicz.
Based on an original story, "The General," by Lajos Biro.

Motion Picture Continuities, edited by Frances Taylor
Patterson. New York: Columbia University Press, 1929,
pp. 157–246.

201   *Last Year at Marienbad (L'Année Dernière à Marienbad)*
Précitel-Terrafilm, 1961.
Directed by Alain Resnais.
Original screenplay by Alain Robbe-Grillet.
Last Year at Marienbad, by Alain Robbe-Grillet. New York:
Grove Press, 1962, 168 pp. London: Calder and Boyars,
1962, 151 pp.
Elements of Film, by Lee R. Bobker. New York: Harcourt,
Brace & World, 1969, pp. 44–46 (excerpt).

202   *The Lavender Hill Mob*
Ealing Studios, 1951.
Directed by Charles Crichton.
Original screenplay by T. E. B. Clarke.
The Cinema 1952, edited by Roger Manvell and R. K. Neilson
Baxter. Harmondsworth, Middlesex: Penguin Books,
1952, pp. 32–51 (excerpt).

203   *Let There Be Light*
United States Army, 1946 (documentary).
Directed by John Huston.
Script by Charles Kaufman.
Film: Book 2, edited by Robert Hughes. New York: Grove
Press, 1962, pp. 205–233.

204   *Les Liaisons Dangereuses*
Les Films Marceau-Cocinor, 1959.
Directed by Roger Vadim.

Screenplay by Roger Vailland, Roger Vadim and Claude Brulé.
Based on the novel by Choderlos de Laclos.

Les Liaisons Dangereuses, by Roger Vailland, Roger Vadim
and Claude Brulé. New York: Ballantine Books, 1962, 256 pp.

The Moving Image, by Robert Gessner. New York: E. P.
Dutton & Co., 1968, pp. 373–374 (excerpt).

205　*Life of an American Fireman*
Edison, 1903 (short).
Directed by Edwin S. Porter.
Original scenario by Edwin S. Porter.

First published in the Edison Catalogue of 1903.

The Rise of the American Film, by Lewis Jacobs. New York:
Harcourt, Brace and Company, 1939, pp. 38–41.

The Emergence of Film Art, by Lewis Jacobs. New York:
Hopkinson and Blake, 1969, pp. 23–25.

206　*The Life of Emile Zola*
Warner Bros., 1937.
Directed by William Dieterle.
Screenplay by Norman Reilly Raine, Heinz Herald and
Geza Herczeg.

Based on an original story by Heinz Herald and Geza Herczeg,
and the book *Zola and His Times* by Matthew Josephson.

Twenty Best Film Plays, edited by John Gassner and Dudley
Nichols. New York: Crown Publishers, 1943, pp. 653–704.

Great Film Plays, edited by John Gassner and Dudley Nichols.
New York: Crown Publishers, 1959, pp. 119–170.

207　*A Light Woman*
Gainsborough, 1928.
Directed by Adrian Brunel.

Scenario by Adrian Brunel and Angus MacPhail.
Based on an original story by Dale Laurence.
Filmcraft, by Adrian Brunel. London: George Newnes, 1936,
pp. 141–152 (excerpts).

208   *The Lion in Winter*
Avco Embassy, 1968.
Directed by Anthony Harvey.
Screenplay by James Goldman, based on his play.
The Lion in Winter, by James Goldman. New York: Dell
Publishing Co., 1968, 139 pp.

209   *Little Caesar*
First National, 1930.
Directed by Mervyn LeRoy.
Screenplay by Francis Edwards Faragoh.
Based on the novel by W. R. Burnett.
Twenty Best Film Plays, edited by John Gassner and Dudley
Nichols. New York: Crown Publishers, 1943, pp. 477–520.

210   *Little Fauss and Big Halsy*
Alfran-Furie/Paramount, 1970.
Directed by Sidney J. Furie.
Original screenplay by Charles Eastman.
Little Fauss and Big Halsy, by Charles Eastman. New York:
Farrar, Straus and Giroux, 1970, 164 pp.

211   *Little Women*
RKO Radio, 1933.
Directed by George Cukor.

Screenplay by Sarah Y. Mason and Victor Heerman.
Based on the novel by Louisa May Alcott.

Four-Star Scripts, edited by Lorraine Noble. Garden City:
   Doubleday, Doran & Company, 1936, pp. 213–319.

212   *The Lost Weekend*
Paramount, 1945.
Directed by Billy Wilder.
Screenplay by Charles Brackett and Billy Wilder.
Based on the novel by Charles Jackson.

Best Film Plays–1945, edited by John Gassner and Dudley
   Nichols. New York: Crown Publishers, 1946, pp. 1–56.

213   *The Lost World*
First National, 1925.
Directed by Harry O. Hoyt and Willis H. O'Brien.
Scenario by Marion Fairfax.
Based on the novel by Sir Arthur Conan Doyle.

Classic Film Collector, No. 23 (Spring 1969), pp. 22–23;
   No. 24 (Summer 1969), pp. 28–31; No. 25 (Fall 1969)
   pp. 21–24; No. 26 (Winter 1970), pp. 17–20; No. 27
   (Spring-Summer 1970), pp. 17–20; No. 28 (Fall 1970),
   pp. 17–20.

214   *The Love Expert*
First National, 1920.
Directed by David Kirkland.
Original scenario by John Emerson and Anita Loos.

How to Write Photoplays, by John Emerson and Anita Loos.
   New York: The James A. McCann Company, 1920,
   pp. 108–154.

215　*Love Finds Andy Hardy*
Metro-Goldwyn-Mayer, 1938.
Directed by George B. Seitz.
Screenplay by William Ludwig.
From the stories by Vivien R. Bretherton.
Based on the characters created by Aurania Rouverol.

Foremost Films of 1938, by Frank Vreeland. New York and
　Chicago: Pitman Publishing Corporation, 1939, pp. 114–128
　(excerpts).

216　*Love Incog.*
Produced under another title (short).
Directed by Eustace Hale Ball.
Original scenario by Eustace Hale Ball.

The Art of the Photoplay, by Eustace Hale Ball. New York:
　G. W. Dillingham Company, 1913, pp. 85–99.

217　*The Lure of the Rose*
Directed by J. Arthur Nelson.
Original scenario by J. Arthur Nelson.

The Photo-Play, by J. Arthur Nelson. Los Angeles: Photoplay
　Publishing Company, 1913 (Second edition), insert between
　pp. 224 and 225.

218　*M*
Nero Film, 1931.
Directed by Fritz Lang.
Screenplay by Thea von Harbou.
Based on an article by Egon Jacobson.

M, by Fritz Lang. London: Lorrimer Publishing, 1968, 108 pp.
　New York: Simon and Schuster, 1968, 108 pp.

219 *Made in U. S. A.*
Rome-Paris Films, 1967.
Directed by Jean-Luc Godard.
Screenplay by Jean-Luc Godard.
Based on the novel *The Jugger* by Richard Stark (pseud. of
Donald E. Westlake).
Made in USA, by Jean-Luc Godard. London: Lorrimer
Publishing, 1967, 87 pp.
Jean-Luc Godard, by Jean Collet. New York: Crown
Publishers, 1970, pp. 135–138 (excerpt).

220 *The Magician* (*Ansiktet*)
Svensk Filmindustri, 1958.
Directed by Ingmar Bergman.
Original screenplay by Ingmar Bergman.
Four Screenplays of Ingmar Bergman. New York: Simon and
Schuster, 1960, pp. 241–325.
The Moving Image, by Robert Gessner. New York: E. P. Dutton
& Co., 1968, pp. 208–211 (excerpts).

221 *The Magnificent Ambersons*
Mercury/RKO Radio, 1942.
Directed by Orson Welles.
Screenplay by Orson Welles.
Based on the novel by Booth Tarkington.
The Cinema of Orson Welles, by Peter Cowie. London:
A. Zwemmer, 1965, pp. 77–82 (excerpts). New York: A. S.
Barnes & Co., 1965, pp. 77–82 (excerpts).

222 *Major Barbara*
London Films, 1941.
Directed by Gabriel Pascal.
Screenplay by Bernard Shaw, based on his play.

Major Barbara, by Bernard Shaw. Baltimore: Penguin Books, 1951, 160 pp.

223   *Make Way for Tomorrow*
Paramount, 1937.
Directed by Leo McCarey.
Screenplay by Viña Delmar.
Based on the novel *Years Are So Long* by Josephine Lawrence, and a play by Helen and Nolan Leary.
Twenty Best Film Plays, edited by John Gassner and Dudley Nichols. New York: Crown Publishers, 1943, pp. 433–476.

224   *A Man in the Open*
United Picture Theatres, 1919.
Directed by Ernest C. Warde.
Scenario by Fred Myton.
Based on the novel by Roger Pocock.
Photoplay Writing, by William Lord Wright. New York: Falk Publishing Co., 1922, pp. 87–105 (excerpts).

225   *The Man Who Could Work Miracles*
London Films, 1936.
Directed by Lothar Mendes.
Screenplay by H. G. Wells, based on his story.
Man Who Could Work Miracles, by H. G. Wells. London and New York: The Macmillan Company, 1936, 109 pp.

226   *The Manchurian Candidate*
M. C. Productions/United Artists, 1962.
Directed by John Frankenheimer.

Screenplay by George Axelrod.
Based on the novel by Richard Condon.
The Cinema of John Frankenheimer, by Gerald Pratley.
   London: A. Zwemmer, 1969, pp. 94–96 (excerpt). New
   York: A. S. Barnes & Co., 1969, pp. 94–96 (excerpt).

227   *La Mandragola* (*The Mandrake*)
Arco Film–Lux Cie de France, 1966.
Directed by Alberto Lattuada.
Screenplay by Luigi Magni, Stefano Strucchi and Alberto
   Lattuada.
Based on the play by Niccolò Machiavelli.
The Moving Image, by Robert Gessner. New York: E. P. Dutton
   & Co., 1968, pp. 370–372 (excerpt).

228   *A Man's a Man*
Produced under another title (short).
Original scenario by James Slevin.
On Picture-Play Writing: A Handbook of Workmanship, by
   James Slevin. Cedar Grove, New Jersey: Farmer Smith,
   1912, pp. 68–84.

229   *Man's Fate*
Unproduced.
Screenplay by James Agee.
Based on the novel by André Malraux.
Films, I, No. 1 (November 1939), 51–60 (excerpt).
The Collected Short Prose of James Agee. Boston: Houghton
   Mifflin Company, 1968, pp. 205–217 (excerpt).

230   *The Married Woman* (*La Femme Mariée*)
Anouchka Films-Orsay Films, 1964.
Directed by Jean-Luc Godard.
Original screenplay by Jean-Luc Godard.
The Married Woman, by Jean-Luc Godard. New York: Berkley
   Publishing Corporation, 1965, 160 pp. (text based on the
   English subtitles of Ursule Molinaro).

231   *Masculine Feminine* (*Masculin-Féminin*)
Argos-Svenskfilmindustri-Sandrews-Anouchka, 1966.
Directed by Jean-Luc Godard.
Screenplay by Jean-Luc Godard.
Based on the stories "Paul's Mistress" and "The Signal"
   by Guy de Maupassant.
Masculine Feminine, by Jean-Luc Godard. New York:
   Grove Press, 1969, 288 pp.

232   *A Medal for Benny*
Paramount, 1945.
Directed by Irving Pichel.
Screenplay by Frank Butler.
Additional dialogue by Jack Wagner.
Based on an unpublished story by John Steinbeck and
   Jack Wagner.
Best Film Plays—1945, edited by John Gassner and Dudley
   Nichols. New York: Crown Publishers, 1946, pp. 589–648.
The Screen Writer, I, No. 2 (July 1945), 8–14 (excerpt).

233   *Michael and Mary*
Gainsborough, 1931.
Directed by Victor Saville.

Screenplay by Angus MacPhail and Robert Stevenson.
Based on the play by A. A. Milne.
Films: The Way of the Cinema, by Andrew Buchanan. London:
Sir Isaac Pitman & Sons, 1932, pp. 110–112 (excerpts).

234   *A Midnight Cupid*
Biograph, 1910 (short).
Original scenario by Stanner E. V. Taylor.
Motion Picture Work, by David Sherill Hulfish. Chicago:
American School of Correspondence, 1913, Vol. 2, pp. 79–82.

235   *The Mighty Barnum*
20th Century/United Artists, 1934.
Directed by Walter Lang.
Original screenplay by Gene Fowler and Bess Meredyth.
The Mighty Barnum, by Gene Fowler and Bess Meredyth.
New York: Covici-Friede, 1934, 240 pp.

236   *Mine Own Executioner*
London Films, 1947.
Directed by Anthony Kimmins.
Screenplay by Nigel Balchin, based on his novel.
From Script to Screen, by Bruce Woodhouse. London:
Winchester Publications, 1948, pp. 179–186 (excerpt).

237   *Miracle in Milan (Miracolo a Milano)*
Produzioni De Sica–Ente Nazionale Industrie Cinematografiche,
1950.
Directed by Vittorio De Sica.
Screenplay by Cesare Zavattini and Vittorio De Sica, with
Suso Cecchi d'Amico, Mario Chiari and Adolfo Franci.
Based on the novel *Totò, il Buono* by Cesare Zavattini.

Miracle in Milan, by Vittorio De Sica. New York: The Orion Press, 1968, 120 pp. Baltimore: Penguin Books, 1969, 120 pp.

238   *The Miracle of Morgan's Creek*
Paramount, 1944.
Directed by Preston Sturges.
Original screenplay by Preston Sturges.
Best Film Plays of 1943–1944, edited by John Gassner and Dudley Nichols. New York: Crown Publishers, 1945, pp. 223–298.

239   *The Misfits*
Seven Arts/United Artists, 1961.
Directed by John Huston.
Screenplay by Arthur Miller, based on his story.
The Misfits, by Arthur Miller. New York: The Viking Press, 1961, 132 pp. London: Secker & Warburg, 1961, 132 pp. New York: Dell Publishing Co., 1961, 223 pp. London: Penguin Books, 1961, 141 pp.

240   *Mr. Smith Goes to Washington*
Columbia, 1939.
Directed by Frank Capra.
Screenplay by Sidney Buchman.
(Contributor to screenplay construction and dialogue: Myles Connolly.)
Based on an original story by Lewis R. Foster.
Twenty Best Film Plays, edited by John Gassner and Dudley Nichols. New York: Crown Publishers, 1943, pp. 583–651.
The Best Pictures, 1939–1940, edited by Jerry Wald and Richard Macaulay. New York: Dodd, Mead & Company, 1940, pp. 189–239 (excerpts).

241 *Mrs. Miniver*
Metro-Goldwyn-Mayer, 1942.
Directed by William Wyler.
Screenplay by Arthur Wimperis, George Froeschel,
James Hilton and Claudine West.
(Contributors to screenplay: R. C. Sherriff and Paul Osborn.)
Based on the novel by Jan Struther.
Twenty Best Film Plays, edited by John Gassner and Dudley
Nichols. New York: Crown Publishers, 1943, pp. 771–832.

242 *The More the Merrier*
Columbia, 1943.
Directed by George Stevens.
Screenplay by Robert Russell, Frank Ross, Richard Flournoy
and Lewis R. Foster.
Based on an original story by Robert Russell and Frank Ross.
Best Film Plays of 1943–1944, edited by John Gassner and
Dudley Nichols. New York: Crown Publishers, 1945,
pp. 451–509.

243 *A Mother's Trust*
Majestic, 1914 (short).
Directed by Donald Crisp.
Original scenario by Russell E. Smith.
How to Write a Photoplay, by Arthur Winfield Thomas.
Chicago: Photoplaywrights Association of America,
1914, pp. 83–88.

244 *Munitions* (episode from *The March of Time*, Vol. 1,
No. 3)
Time, Inc./RKO Radio, 1935 (documentary short).

One-Reel Scenarios for Amateur Movie-Makers, edited by
   Margaret Mayorga. New York: Samuel French,
   1938, pp. 179–182.

245 *Murder in the Cathedral*
George Hoellering, 1951.
Directed by George Hoellering.
Screenplay by T. S. Eliot, based on his play.
The Film of Murder in the Cathedral, by T. S. Eliot and
   George Hoellering. London: Faber & Faber, 1952, 110 pp.
   New York: Harcourt, Brace and Company, 1952, 110 pp.

246 *My Man Godfrey*
Universal, 1936.
Directed by Gregory La Cava.
Screenplay by Morrie Ryskind and Eric Hatch.
Based on the novel by Eric Hatch.
Twenty Best Film Plays, edited by John Gassner and Dudley
   Nichols. New York: Crown Publishers, 1943, pp. 131–179.

247 *Native Land*
Frontier Films, 1942.
Directed by Leo Hurwitz and Paul Strand.
Original screenplay by David Wolff, Leo Hurwitz and
   Paul Strand.
Commentary by David Wolff.
Based on material of the United States Senate Civil Liberties
   Committee and other public documents.
New Fields for the Writer, edited by Stephen Moore. New York:
   National Library Press, 1939, pp. 89–97 (excerpt, as
   "Frontier Films' Production No. 5").

248   *Nazarín*
Manuel Barbachano Ponce, 1959.
Directed by Luis Buñuel.
Screenplay by Luis Buñuel and Julio Alejandro.
Based on the novel by Benito Pérez Galdós.
Luis Buñuel, by Ado Kyrou. New York: Simon and Schuster,
   1963, pp. 160–164 (excerpts).

249   *Night and Fog* (*Nuit et Brouillard*)
Argos Film-Como Film, 1955 (short).
Directed by Alain Resnais.
Script by Jean Cayrol.
Based on *The Tragedy of the Deportations* by André Michel
   and Olga Wormser.
Film: Book 2, edited by Robert Hughes. New York: Grove
   Press, 1962, pp. 234–255.

250   *The Night of the Hunter*
Paul Gregory/United Artists, 1955.
Directed by Charles Laughton.
Screenplay by James Agee.
Based on the novel by Davis Grubb.
Agee on Film, Volume Two, by James Agee. New York:
   McDowell, Obolensky, 1960, pp. 261–354. Boston: Beacon
   Press, 1964, pp. 261–354. New York: Grosset & Dunlap,
   1969, pp. 261–354.

251   *The Night of the Iguana*
Metro-Goldwyn-Mayer–Seven Arts, 1964.
Directed by John Huston.
Screenplay by Anthony Veiller and John Huston.
Based on the play by Tennessee Williams.

The Moving Image, by Robert Gessner. New York: E. P. Dutton & Co., 1968, pp. 224–227, 230–233 (excerpts).

252 *The Nights of Cabiria* (*Le Notti di Cabiria*)
Dino De Laurentiis, 1957.
Directed by Federico Fellini.
Original screenplay by Federico Fellini, Ennio Flaiano and Tullio Pinelli.
Additional dialogue by Pier Paolo Pasolini.
Federico Fellini, by Gilbert Salachas. New York: Crown Publishers, 1969, pp. 135–148 (excerpts).

253 *Ninotchka*
Metro-Goldwyn-Mayer, 1939.
Directed by Ernst Lubitsch.
Screenplay by Charles Brackett, Billy Wilder and Walter Reisch.
Based on an original story by Melchior Lengyel.
The Best Pictures, 1939–1940, edited by Jerry Wald and Richard Macaulay. New York: Dodd, Mead & Company, 1940, pp. 79–128 (excerpts).
The Lubitsch Touch, by Herman G. Weinberg. New York: E. P. Dutton & Co., 1968, pp. 170–202 (excerpts).

254 *Noa Noa*
Unproduced.
Original screenplay by James Agee.
Agee on Film, Volume Two, by James Agee. New York: McDowell, Obolensky, 1960, pp. 1–147. Boston: Beacon Press, 1964, pp. 1–147. New York: Grosset & Dunlap, 1969, pp. 1–147.
Film: Book 1, edited by Robert Hughes. New York: Grove Press, 1959, pp. 109–121 (excerpts).

255   *None But the Lonely Heart*
RKO Radio, 1944.
Directed by Clifford Odets.
Screenplay by Clifford Odets.
Based on the novel by Richard Llewellyn.
Best Film Plays—1945, edited by John Gassner and Dudley
   Nichols. New York: Crown Publishers, 1946, pp. 261–330.

256   *The North Star*
Samuel Goldwyn/RKO Radio, 1943.
Directed by Lewis Milestone.
Original screenplay by Lillian Hellman.
The North Star, by Lillian Hellman. New York: The Viking
   Press, 1943, 118 pp.

257   *Nosferatu*
Prana-Film, 1922.
Directed by F. W. Murnau.
Scenario by Henrik Galeen.
Based on the novel *Dracula* by Bram Stoker.
Films of Tyranny, by Richard B. Byrne. Madison, Wisconsin:
   College Printing & Typing Co., 1966, pp. 97–148
   (shot analysis).

258   *La Notte* (*The Night*)
Nepi-Film–Silva Film–Sofitedip, 1961.
Directed by Michelangelo Antonioni.
Original screenplay by Michelangelo Antonioni, Ennio
   Flaiano and Tonino Guerra.
Screenplays of Michelangelo Antonioni. New York: The Orion
   Press, 1963, pp. 209–276.

Michelangelo Antonioni, by Pierre Leprohon. New York: Simon and Schuster, 1963, pp. 140–146 (excerpt).

259 *Odd Man Out*
Two Cities, 1947.
Directed by Carol Reed.
Screenplay by F. L. Green and R. C. Sherriff.
Based on the novel by F. L. Green.
Three British Screen Plays, edited by Roger Manvell. London: Methuen & Co., 1950, pp. 83–202.

260 *Of Mice and Men*
Hal Roach/United Artists, 1940.
Directed by Lewis Milestone.
Screenplay by Eugene Solow.
Based on the novel and play by John Steinbeck.
The Moving Image, by Robert Gessner. New York: E. P. Dutton & Co., 1968, pp. 88–92 (excerpts).

261 *Ohm's Law*
U. S. Army Pictorial Center, 19?? (short).
Script by Paul Caster.
Audiovisual Script Writing, by Norton S. Parker. New Brunswick: Rutgers University Press, 1968, pp. 135–184.

262 *Old and New* (*The General Line*)
Sovkino, 1929.
Directed by Sergei M. Eisenstein and Grigori Alexandrov.
Original scenario by Sergei M. Eisenstein and Grigori Alexandrov.
Film Writing Forms, edited by Lewis Jacobs. New York: Gotham Book Mart, 1934, pp. 25–39, 61.

263   *One of Us*
Unproduced.
Scenario by Henry Albert Phillips.
Based on the play by Jack Lait.
(Another version, scripted by Walter Woods, was filmed in
   1919 as *The Love Burglar*.)
The Feature Photoplay, by Henry Albert Phillips. Springfield,
   Mass.: The Home Correspondence School, 1921,
   pp. 267–273 (excerpt).

264   *Orpheus* (*Orphée*)
André Paulvé, 1950.
Directed by Jean Cocteau.
Screenplay by Jean Cocteau, from his play, based on the
   Greek legend.
Jean Cocteau, by René Gilson. New York: Crown Publishers,
   1969, pp. 131–143 (excerpts).

265   *Our Country*
Strand Films, 1944 (documentary).
Directed by John Eldridge.
Commentary by Dylan Thomas.
Documentary News Letter, V, No. 49 (1945), 96 (excerpt).

266   *Our Hospitality*
Joseph M. Schenck/Metro, 1923.
Directed by Buster Keaton and John G. Blystone.
Original scenario by Jean Havez, Joseph Mitchell and
   Clyde Bruckman.
Buster Keaton, by David Robinson. London: Secker & Warburg,
   1969, pp. 91–94 (excerpt). Bloomington: Indiana University
   Press, 1969, pp. 91–94 (excerpt).

267 *The Outrage*
Metro-Goldwyn-Mayer, 1964.
Directed by Martin Ritt.
Screenplay by Michael Kanin.
Based on the stories "Rashomon" and "In the Grove" by
    Ryunosuke Akutagawa, the film *Rashomon* by Akira
    Kurosawa, and the play *Rashomon* by Fay and Michael Kanin.
Rashomon, by Akira Kurosawa. New York: Grove Press, 1969,
    pp. 243–254 (excerpt).

268 *Over 21*
Sidney Buchman/Columbia, 1945.
Directed by Charles Vidor.
Screenplay by Sidney Buchman.
Based on the play by Ruth Gordon.
Best Film Plays—1945, edited by John Gassner and Dudley
    Nichols. New York: Crown Publishers, 1946, pp. 521–588.

269 *The Ox-Bow Incident*
Twentieth Century-Fox, 1942.
Directed by William A. Wellman.
Screenplay by Lamar Trotti.
Based on the novel by Walter Van Tilburg Clark.
Best Film Plays of 1943–1944, edited by John Gassner and
    Dudley Nichols. New York: Crown Publishers, 1945,
    pp. 511–560.
The Moving Image, by Robert Gessner. New York: E. P. Dutton
    & Co., 1968, pp. 302–303 (excerpt).

270 *Paisan*
Organizzazione Films Internazionali, 1946.
Directed by Roberto Rossellini.

Original screenplay by Sergio Amidei, Federico Fellini and
Roberto Rossellini, with the collaboration of Alfred Hayes,
Klauss Mann and Marcello Pagliero.
English narration by Stuart Legg and Raymond Spottiswoode.
Film Culture, No. 31 (Winter 1963–64), pp. 61–67 (excerpts).

271 *Pardon Me, Sir, But Is My Eye Hurting Your Elbow?*
Unproduced.
Pardon Me, Sir, But Is My Eye Hurting Your Elbow? by
Gregory Corso, Bruce Jay Friedman, Allen Ginsberg, Herbert
Gold, Arthur Kopit, Jack Richardson, Philip Roth, Robert
Paul Smith, Terry Southern, Arnold Weinstein, and Bob
Booker & George Foster. New York: Bernard Geis Associates,
1968, 173 pp.

272 *Peter Pan*
Unproduced.
Scenario by James M. Barrie, based on his play.
Fifty Years of Peter Pan, by Roger Lancelyn Green.
London: Peter Davies, 1954, pp. 171–218.

273 *Le Petit Soldat* (*The Little Soldier*)
Georges de Beauregard Société Nouvelle de Cinéma, 1963.
Directed by Jean-Luc Godard.
Original screenplay by Jean-Luc Godard.
Le Petit Soldat, by Jean-Luc Godard. London: Lorrimer
Publishing, 1967, 95 pp.

274 *Pierrot le Fou*
Rome-Paris Films/Dino de Laurentiis Cinematographica, 1965.
Directed by Jean-Luc Godard.

Screenplay by Jean-Luc Godard.

Based on the novel *Obsession* by Lionel White.

Pierrot le Fou, by Jean-Luc Godard. London: Lorrimer Publishing, 1969, 104 pp. New York: Simon and Schuster, 1970, 104 pp.

275 *Pirate Gold*

Pathé, 1920 (serial).

Directed by George B. Seitz.

Original scenario by Frank Leon Smith.

Bound and Gagged, by Kalton C. Lahue. South Brunswick and New York: A. S. Barnes and Company, 1968, pp. 319–348 (excerpt: Chapter I).

276 *A Place in the Sun*

Paramount, 1951.

Directed by George Stevens.

Screenplay by Michael Wilson and Harry Brown.

Based on the novel *An American Tragedy* by Theodore Dreiser, and the play by Patrick Kearney.

The Moving Image, by Robert Gessner. New York: E. P. Dutton & Co., 1968, pp. 137–150 (excerpts).

277 *Point of Order!*

Point Films, 1963 (documentary).

Produced by Emile de Antonio and Daniel Talbot from Columbia Broadcasting System television Kinescopes.

Point of Order! by Emile de Antonio and Daniel Talbot. New York: W. W. Norton & Company, 1964, 108 pp.

278 *The Postman Always Rings Twice*
Metro-Goldwyn-Mayer, 1946.
Directed by Tay Garnett.
Screenplay by Harry Ruskin and Niven Busch.
Based on the novel by James M. Cain.
The Moving Image, by Robert Gessner. New York: E. P. Dutton
    & Co., 1968, pp. 36–37 (excerpt).

279 *The Prince and the Showgirl*
Marilyn Monroe/Warner Bros., 1957.
Directed by Laurence Olivier.
Screenplay by Terence Rattigan, based on his play
    The Sleeping Prince.
The Prince and the Showgirl, by Terence Rattigan. New York:
    The New American Library (Signet Books), 1957, 127 pp.

280 *The Private Life of Henry VIII*
London Films, 1933.
Directed by Alexander Korda.
Original screenplay by Lajos Biro and Arthur Wimperis.
The Private Life of Henry VIII, edited by Ernest Betts.
    London: Methuen & Co., 1934, 108 pp.
The Moving Image, by Robert Gessner. New York: E. P. Dutton
    & Co., 1968, pp. 304–306 (excerpt).

281 *Professor Mamlock*
Lenfilm, 1938.
Directed by Adolf Minkin and Herbert Rappoport.
Screenplay by Friedrich Wolff, Adolf Minkin and
    Herbert Rappoport.
Based on the play by Friedrich Wolff.

One Act Play Magazine, II, No. 5 (November 1938),
489–495 (excerpt).

282   *Pull My Daisy*
G-String Enterprises, 1959 (short).
Directed by Robert Frank and Alfred Leslie.
Original screenplay by Jack Kerouac.
Pull My Daisy, by Jack Kerouac. New York: Grove Press,
1961, 72 pp.

283   *The Purple Heart*
Twentieth Century-Fox, 1944.
Directed by Lewis Milestone.
Screenplay by Jerome Cady.
Based on an original story by Melville Crossman.
Best Film Plays of 1943–1944, edited by John Gassner and
Dudley Nichols. New York: Crown Publishers, 1945,
pp. 89–148.

284   *Pygmalion*
Gabriel Pascal/Metro-Goldwyn-Mayer, 1938.
Directed by Anthony Asquith and Leslie Howard.
Screenplay by Bernard Shaw.
Adaptation by W. P. Lipscomb, Cecil Lewis and Ian Dalrymple.
Based on the play by Bernard Shaw.
Pygmalion, by Bernard Shaw. Baltimore: Penguin Books,
1951, 125 pp.
The Serpent's Eye, by Donald P. Costello. Notre Dame:
University of Notre Dame Press, 1965, pp. 165–188
(excerpt).
The Moving Image, by Robert Gessner. New York: E. P. Dutton
& Co., 1968, pp. 109–114, 319–321, 363–366 (excerpts).

285　*Quantrill's Raiders*
Allied Artists, 1958.
Directed by Edward Bernds.
Original screenplay by Polly James.
The Moving Image, by Robert Gessner. New York:
　　E. P. Dutton & Co., 1968, pp. 354–356 (excerpt).

286　*Quartet*
Gainsborough, 1948.
Part I: "The Facts of Life". Directed by Ralph Smart.
Part II: "The Alien Corn". Directed by Harold French.
Part III: "The Kite". Directed by Arthur Crabtree.
Part IV: "The Colonel's Lady". Directed by Ken Annakin.
Screenplays by R. C. Sherriff.
Based on the stories by W. Somerset Maugham.

Quartet, by W. Somerset Maugham and R. C. Sherriff. London:
　　William Heinemann, 1948, 243 pp. Garden City: Doubleday
　　& Company, 1949, 189 pp.
A College Treasury, edited by Paul A. Jorgensen and Frederick
　　B. Shroyer. New York: Charles Scribner's Sons, 1956, Vol. 2,
　　pp. 393–407 ("The Colonel's Lady" only).

287　*Que Viva Mexico!*
Upton Sinclair, 1931 (unfinished).
Directed by Sergei M. Eisenstein and Grigori Alexandrov.
Original screenplay by Sergei M. Eisenstein and Grigori
　　Alexandrov.
[Though never released as Eisenstein conceived it, a large
　　portion appeared as *Thunder Over Mexico* (1933).
　　Other portions were compiled into two shorts, *Death Day*
　　and *Time in the Sun.*]

Experimental Cinema, I, No. 5 (1934), 5–13, 52.

Que Viva Mexico! by S. M. Eisenstein. London: Vision Press, 1952, 89 pp.

Sergei Eisenstein, by Léon Moussinac. New York: Crown Publishers, 1970, pp. 128–141 (excerpts).

288 *Rashomon*

Daiei, 1950.

Directed by Akira Kurosawa.

Screenplay by Shinobu Hashimoto and Akira Kurosawa.

Based on the stories "Rashomon" and "In the Grove" by Ryunosuke Akutagawa.

Rashomon, by Akira Kurosawa. New York: Grove Press, 1969, 255 pp.

289 *Rebecca*

Selznick International/United Artists, 1940.

Directed by Alfred Hitchcock.

Screenplay by Robert E. Sherwood and Joan Harrison.

Adaptation by Philip MacDonald and Michael Hogan.

Based on the novel by Daphne du Maurier.

Twenty Best Film Plays, edited by John Gassner and Dudley Nichols. New York: Crown Publishers, 1943, pp. 233–291.

Great Film Plays, edited by John Gassner and Dudley Nichols. New York: Crown Publishers, 1959, pp. 60–118.

The Best Pictures, 1930–1940, edited by Jerry Wald and Richard Macaulay. New York: Dodd, Mead & Company, 1940, pp. 129–187 (excerpts).

290 *Rebecca's Daughters*

Unproduced.

Original screenplay by Dylan Thomas.

Rebecca's Daughters, by Dylan Thomas. London: Triton
Publishing Company, 1965, 144 pp. Boston: Little, Brown
and Company, 1966, 144 pp.

291   *The Red Badge of Courage*
Metro-Goldwyn-Mayer, 1951.
Directed by John Huston.
Screenplay by John Huston.
Adaptation by Albert Band.
Based on the novel by Stephen Crane.
The Moving Image, by Robert Gessner. New York: E. P. Dutton
& Co., 1968, pp. 59–61 (excerpts).

292   *Red Hot Romance*
First National, 1921.
Directed by Victor Fleming.
Original scenario by John Emerson and Anita Loos.
Breaking Into the Movies, by John Emerson and Anita Loos.
New York: The James A. McCann Company, 1921,
pp. 55–115.

293   *The Revolt of the Machines*
Unproduced.
Original scenario by Romain Rolland.
The Revolt of the Machines, by Romain Rolland. Ithaca,
New York: The Dragon Press, 1932, 57 pp.
Cinemages, No. 9 (August 1, 1958), pp. 57–70.

294   *Rocco and His Brothers* (*Rocco e i Suoi Fratelli*)
Titanus–Les Films Marceau, 1960.
Directed by Luchino Visconti.

Screenplay by Luchino Visconti, Suso Cecchi d'Amico,
   Pasquale Festa Campanile, Massimo Franciosa and
   Enrico Medioli.
From a story by Luchino Visconti, Vasco Pratolini and
   Suso Cecchi d'Amico.
Based on the book *Il Ponte della Ghisolfa* (*The Bridge of
   Ghisolfa*) by Giovanni Testori.
Three Screenplays, by Luchino Visconti. New York: The
   Orion Press, 1970, pp. 93–271.
Films and Filming, VII, No. 12 (September 1961),
   19–21, 42 (excerpt).

295   *Romeo and Juliet*
Metro-Goldwyn-Mayer, 1936.
Directed by George Cukor.
Screenplay adapted by Talbot Jennings.
From the play by William Shakespeare.
Romeo and Juliet, by William Shakespeare. New York: Random
   House, 1936, pp. 139–229. London: Arthur Barker, 1936,
   pp. 139–229.

296   *Round Trip: The U. S. A. in World Trade*
The World Today/Twentieth Century Fund, 1947
   (documentary).
The Information Film, by Gloria Waldron. New York:
   Columbia University Press, 1949, pp. 217–225 (excerpts).

297   *Ruggles of Red Gap*
Paramount, 1935.
Directed by Leo McCarey.
Screenplay by Walter DeLeon and Harlan Thompson.
Adaptation by Humphrey Pearson.

(Contributor to treatment: Garnett Weston. Contributors to
adaptation: Jack Cunningham and William Slavens McNutt.
Contributor on special sequences: Arthur MacRae.)
Based on the novel and play by Harry Leon Wilson.
The Moving Image, by Robert Gessner. New York: E. P. Dutton
& Co., 1968, pp. 357–359 (excerpt).

298   *The Rules of the Game* (*La Règle du Jeu*)
La Nouvelle Edition Française, 1939.
Directed by Jean Renoir.
Original screenplay by Jean Renoir.
The Rules of the Game, by Jean Renoir. London: Lorrimer
Publishing, 1970, 168 pp. New York: Simon and Schuster,
1970, 168 pp.

299   *Saint Joan*
Unproduced.
Screenplay by Bernard Shaw, based on his play.
(Another version, scripted by Graham Greene, was
filmed in 1957.)
Saint Joan, by Bernard Shaw. Seattle: University of Washington
Press, 1968, 162 pp.

300   *Salesman*
Maysles Brothers, 1969 (documentary).
Salesman, by Albert and David Maysles and Charlotte Zwerin.
New York: The New American Library (Signet Books),
1969, 128 pp.

301   *Salt of the Earth*
Independent Productions, 1954.

Directed by Herbert J. Biberman.
Original screenplay by Michael Wilson.
The California Quarterly, II, No. 4 (Summer 1953), 3–59.
Salt of the Earth: The Story of a Film, by Herbert Biberman.
   Boston: Beacon Press, 1965, pp. 315–373.

302   *Satan McAllister's Heir*
Domino, 1915 (short).
Directed by Walter Edwards.
Original scenario by C. Gardner Sullivan and Thomas H. Ince.
Spellbound in Darkness, by George C. Pratt. Rochester, New
   York: University School of Liberal and Applied Studies, The
   University of Rochester, 1966, Vol. 1, pp. 135–155.

303   *The Scarlet Letter*
Metro-Goldwyn-Mayer, 1926.
Directed by Victor Seastrom.
Scenario by Frances Marion.
Based on the novel by Nathaniel Hawthorne.
Motion Picture Continuities, edited by Frances Taylor Patterson.
   New York: Columbia University Press, 1929, pp. 89–156.

304   *Scenario*
Unproduced.
Scenario by Henry Miller.
Inspired by *The House of Incest* by Anaïs Nin.
Scenario, by Henry Miller. Paris: Obelisk Press, 1937, 40 pp.
The Cosmological Eye, by Henry Miller. Norfolk, Conn.:
   New Directions, 1939, pp. 75–106.
Cinemages, No. 9 (August 1, 1958), pp. 39–56.

305 *Scott of the Antarctic*
Ealing Studios, 1948.
Directed by Charles Frend.
Original screenplay by Walter Meade and Ivor Montagu.
Additional dialogue by Mary Hayley Bell.
Three British Screen Plays, edited by Roger Manvell.
London: Methuen & Co., 1950, pp. 203–299.

306 *The Second Mrs. Tanqueray*
Grand Ideal, 1916.
Directed by Fred Paul.
Scenario by Benedict James.
Based on the play by Sir Arthur Wing Pinero.
Picture Plays and How to Write Them, by J. Farquharson.
London: Hodder and Stoughton, 1916, pp. 77–163.

307 *Secret People*
Ealing Studios, 1951.
Directed by Thorold Dickinson.
Screenplay by Thorold Dickinson and Wolfgang Wilhelm.
Additional dialogue by Christianna Brand.
Based on an original story by Thorold Dickinson, "with
    acknowledgments to Joyce Cary."
Making a Film, edited by Lindsay Anderson. London: George
    Allen and Unwin, 1952, pp. 131–199. New York: The
    Macmillan Company, 1952, pp. 131–199.
The Cinema 1952, edited by Roger Manvell and R. K. Neilson
    Baxter. Harmondsworth, Middlesex: Penguin Books,
    1952, pp. 89–99 (excerpt).

308 *Senso*
Lux Film, 1954.
Directed by Luchino Visconti.

Screenplay by Luchino Visconti and Suso Cecchi d'Amico,
  assisted by Giorgio Prosperi, Carlo Alianello and
  Giorgio Bassani.
English dialogue by Tennessee Williams and Paul Bowles.
Based on the story by Camillo Boito.
Two Screenplays, by Luchino Visconti. New York: The Orion
  Press, 1970, pp. 103–186.

309 *The Seventh Seal (Det Sjunde Inseglet)*
Svensk Filmindustri, 1956.
Directed by Ingmar Bergman.
Original screenplay by Ingmar Bergman.
Four Screenplays of Ingmar Bergman. New York: Simon and
  Schuster, 1960, pp. 95–164.
The Seventh Seal, by Ingmar Bergman. London: Lorrimer
  Publishing, 1968, 82 pp. New York: Simon and Schuster,
  1968, 82 pp.
The Moving Image, by Robert Gessner. New York: E. P. Dutton
  & Co., 1968, pp. 203–207 (excerpts).
Elements of Film, by Lee R. Bobker. New York: Harcourt,
  Brace & World, 1969, pp. 20–22, 144–150 (excerpts).

310 *Shadows*
British and Colonial, 1915 (short).
Directed by Harold Weston.
Original scenario by Harold Weston.
The Art of Photo-Play Writing, by Harold Weston. London:
  McBride, Nast & Co., 1916, pp. 82–114.

311 *Shakespeare's Theater: The Globe Playhouse*
University of California, 1953 (educational short).
Script by William E. Jordan and Mildred R. Jordan.

The Quarterly of Film, Radio, and Television, VIII, No. 4
(Summer 1954), 322–332.

312   *Shanghai Express*
Paramount, 1932.
Directed by Josef von Sternberg.
Screenplay by Jules Furthman.
Based on an original story by Harry Hervey.
Josef von Sternberg, by Herman G. Weinberg. New York:
E. P. Dutton & Co., 1967, pp. 143–162 (excerpts).

313   *The Shell and the Clergyman (La Coquille et le
Clergyman)*
Studio des Ursulines, 1927 (short).
Directed by Germaine Dulac.
Original scenario by Antonin Artaud.
Transition (Paris), No. 19–20 (June 1930), pp. 63–69.

314   *The Sidewalks of New York*
Cinemaplays, 19??
Original scenario by Willard King Bradley.
Inside Secrets of Photoplay Writing, by Willard King Bradley.
New York: Funk & Wagnalls, 1926, pp. 93–181.

315   *The Silence (Tystnaden)*
Svensk Filmindustri, 1963.
Directed by Ingmar Bergman.
Original screenplay by Ingmar Bergman.
A Film Trilogy, by Ingmar Bergman. New York: The Orion
Press, 1967, pp. 105–143. London: Calder and Boyars, 1967,
pp. 105–143.

Three Films by Ingmar Bergman. New York: Grove Press, 1970, pp. 105–143.

316 *Le Silence Est d'Or* (*Man About Town*)
Société Nouvelle Pâthé Cinéma, 1947.
Directed by René Clair.
Original screenplay by René Clair.
English adaptation by Robert Pirosh.
Four Screenplays, by René Clair. New York: The Orion Press, 1970, pp. 1–106.

317 *The Silver Streak*
RKO Radio, 1934.
Directed by Tommy Atkins.
Screenplay by Roger Whately, Jack O'Donnell and H. W. Hanemann.
Based on an original story by Roger Whately.
The Silver Streak, by Roger Whately, Jack O'Donnell and H. W. Hanemann. Los Angeles: Haskell-Travers, 1935, 268 pp.

318 *Simon of the Desert* (*Simon del Desierto*)
Gustavo Alatriste, 1965.
Directed by Luis Buñuel.
Screenplay by Luis Buñuel.
Additional dialogue by Luis Buñuel and Julio Alejandro.
Three Screen Plays, by Luis Buñuel. New York: The Orion Press, 1969, pp. 197–245.

319 *Smiles of a Summer Night* (*Sommarnattens Leende*)
Svensk Filmindustri, 1955.

Directed by Ingmar Bergman.

Original screenplay by Ingmar Bergman.

Four Screenplays of Ingmar Bergman. New York: Simon and
Schuster, 1960, pp. 1–94.

320   *Snow White and the Seven Dwarfs*

Walt Disney/RKO Radio, 1937.

Supervising Director, David Hand.

Story adaptation by Ted Sears, Otto Englander, Earl Hurd,
Dorothy Ann Blank, Richard Creedon, Dick Rickard,
Merrill De Maris and Webb Smith.

Based on the fairy tale by the Brothers Grimm.

Foremost Films of 1938, by Frank Vreeland. New York and
Chicago: Pitman Publishing Corporation, 1939, pp. 49–62
(excerpts).

321   *Some Like It Hot*

Ashton-Mirisch/United Artists, 1959.

Directed by Billy Wilder.

Screenplay by Billy Wilder and I. A. L. Diamond.

Based on an unpublished story by Robert Thoeren and M. Logan.

Some Like It Hot, by Billy Wilder and I. A. L. Diamond. New
York: The New American Library (Signet Books),
1959, 144 pp.

322   *The Southerner*

Loew-Hakim/United Artists, 1945.

Directed by Jean Renoir.

Screenplay by Jean Renoir.

Adaptation by Hugo Butler.

Based on the novel *Hold Autumn in Your Hand* by George
Sessions Perry.

Best Film Plays—1945, edited by John Gassner and Dudley Nichols. New York: Crown Publishers, 1946, pp. 331–380.

323   *The Spanish Dancer*
Famous Players-Lasky/Paramount, 1923.
Directed by Herbert Brenon.
Scenario by June Mathis and Beulah Marie Dix.
Based on the play *Don César de Bazan* by Adolphe D'Ennery (pseud. of Adolphe Philippe) and Dumanoir (pseud. of Philippe François Pinel).
The Spanish Cavalier, by June Mathis. N. p., 1923, 96 pp.

324   *Spellbound*
Selznick International/United Artists, 1945.
Directed by Alfred Hitchcock.
Screenplay by Ben Hecht.
Adaptation by Angus MacPhail.
Based on the novel *The House of Dr. Edwardes* by Francis Beeding.
Best Film Plays—1945, edited by John Gassner and Dudley Nichols. New York: Crown Publishers, 1946, pp. 57–113.

325   *The Spitfire*
Famous Players, 1914.
Scenario by B. P. Schulberg.
Based on the play by Edward Henry Peple.
How to Write a Photoplay, by Arthur Winfield Thomas. Chicago: Photoplaywrights Association of America, 1914, pp. 235–269.

326 *Splendor in the Grass*
NBI/Warner Bros., 1961.
Directed by Elia Kazan.
Original screenplay by William Inge.
Splendor in the Grass, by William Inge. New York:
Bantam Books, 1961, 121 pp.

327 *Stagecoach*
Walter Wanger/United Artists, 1939.
Directed by John Ford.
Screenplay by Dudley Nichols.
Based on the story "Stage to Lordsburg" by Ernest Haycox.
Twenty Best Film Plays, edited by John Gassner and Dudley
Nichols. New York: Crown Publishers, 1943, pp. 995–1038.
Great Film Plays, edited by John Gassner and Dudley Nichols.
New York: Crown Publishers, 1959, pp. 291–334.

328 *Stairway to Heaven* (*A Matter of Life and Death*)
The Archers, 1946.
Directed by Michael Powell and Emeric Pressburger.
Original screenplay by Michael Powell and Emeric Pressburger.
The Moving Image, by Robert Gessner. New York: E. P. Dutton
& Co., 1968, pp. 394–395 (excerpts).

329 *Storm in the West*
Unproduced.
Original screenplay by Sinclair Lewis and Dore Schary.
Storm in the West, by Sinclair Lewis and Dore Schary. New
York: Stein and Day, 1963, 192 pp.

330 *The Story of Louis Pasteur*
Warner Bros., 1936.
Directed by William Dieterle.
Original screenplay by Sheridan Gibney and Pierre Collings.
Four-Star Scripts, edited by Lorraine Noble. Garden City:
Doubleday, Doran & Company, 1936, pp. 320–392.

331 *La Strada*
Ponti-De Laurentiis, 1954.
Directed by Federico Fellini.
Screenplay by Federico Fellini, Ennio Flaiano and Tullio
Pinelli.
Based on an original story by Federico Fellini and
Tullio Pinelli.
Fellini, by Suzanne Budgen. London: British Film Institute,
1966, pp. 103–113 (excerpt).
Federico Fellini, by Gilbert Salachas. New York: Crown
Publishers, 1969, pp. 125–131 (excerpt).

332 *A Streetcar Named Desire*
Charles K. Feldman/Warner Bros., 1951.
Directed by Elia Kazan.
Screenplay by Tennessee Williams.
Adaptation by Oscar Saul.
Based on the play by Tennessee Williams.
The Moving Image, by Robert Gessner. New York: E. P. Dutton
& Co., 1968, pp. 221–224 (excerpts).

333 *Strike*
Goskino-Proletkult, 1925.
Directed by Sergei M. Eisenstein.

Original scenario by Valeri Pletnyov, Sergei M. Eisenstein,
I. Kravchunovsky and Grigori Alexandrov.
The Film Sense, by Sergei M. Eisenstein. New York: Harcourt,
Brace and Company, 1942, pp. 233–235 (excerpt).

334 *Sunset Boulevard*
Paramount, 1950.
Directed by Billy Wilder.
Original screenplay by Charles Brackett, Billy Wilder and
D. M. Marshman, Jr.
The Moving Image, by Robert Gessner. New York: E. P. Dutton
& Co., 1968, pp. 151–160 (excerpts).

335 *Sutter's Gold*
Unproduced.
Scenario by Sergei M. Eisenstein, Grigori Alexandrov and
Ivor Montagu.
Based on the novel by Blaise Cendrars.
(Another version, scripted by Jack Kirkland, Walter Woods
and George O'Neil, was filmed in 1936.)
With Eisenstein in Hollywood, by Ivor Montagu. New York:
International Publishers, 1969, pp. 149–206.
The Film Sense, by Sergei M. Eisenstein. New York: Harcourt,
Brace and Company, 1942, pp. 243–250 (excerpt).

336 *The Swimmer*
Horizon/Columbia, 1968.
Directed by Frank Perry.
Screenplay by Eleanor Perry.
Based on the story by John Cheever.
The Swimmer, by Eleanor Perry. New York: Stein and Day,
1967, 127 pp. New York: Pyramid Books, 1968, 93 pp.

337 *Talents*

Family Films, 1951 (short).

Screenplay by the Screenwriting Class, Cinema Department, University of Southern California.

Based on the story by the Rev. Ernest N. Bigelow.

Writing for the Screen, by Clara Beranger. Dubuque, Iowa: Wm. C. Brown Company, 1950, pp. 179–195.

338 *Telemachus, Friend*

Vitagraph, 1920 (short).

Directed by David Smith.

Scenario by Robert A. Sanborn.

Based on the story by O. Henry (pseud. of William Sydney Porter).

Scenario Writing Today, by Grace Lytton. Boston and New York: Houghton Mifflin Company, 1921, pp. 141–179.

339 *The Temptations of Doctor Antonio* (*Le Tentazioni del Dottor Antonio*) (Part I of *Boccaccio '70*)

Concordia Compagnia Cinematografica-Cineriz-Francinex-Gray Film, 1961.

Directed by Federico Fellini.

Original screenplay by Federico Fellini, Ennio Flaiano and Tullio Pinelli, assisted by Brunello Rondi and Goffredo Parise.

Three Screenplays, by Federico Fellini. New York: The Orion Press, 1970, pp. 253–288.

340 *La Terra Trema*

Universalia, 1947.

Directed by Luchino Visconti.

Original screenplay by Luchino Visconti.

Two Screenplays, by Luchino Visconti. New York: The Orion
Press, 1970, pp. 1–102.

341   *The Testament of Orpheus* (*Le Testament d'Orphée*)
Les Editions Cinégraphiques, 1959.
Directed by Jean Cocteau.
Original screenplay by Jean Cocteau.
Two Screenplays, by Jean Cocteau. New York: The Orion
Press, 1968, pp. 69–144. Baltimore: Penguin Books, 1969,
pp. 69–144. London: Calder and Boyars, 1970, pp. 69–144.
Jean Cocteau, by René Gilson. New York: Crown Publishers,
1969, pp. 143–151 (excerpts).

342   *That Certain Age*
Universal, 1938.
Directed by Edward Ludwig.
Screenplay by Bruce Manning.
Based on an original story by F. Hugh Herbert.
Foremost Films of 1938, by Frank Vreeland. New York and
Chicago: Pitman Publishing Corporation, 1939, pp. 182–198
(excerpts).

343   *They Shoot Horses, Don't They?*
ABC Pictures, 1969.
Directed by Sydney Pollack.
Screenplay by James Poe and Robert E. Thompson.
Based on the novel by Horace McCoy.
They Shoot Horses, Don't They? by Horace McCoy. New York:
Avon Books, 1969, 319 pp. (includes the text of the novel).

344 *Things to Come*
London Films, 1936.
Directed by William Cameron Menzies.
Screenplay by H. G. Wells, based on his book *The Shape of Things to Come.*
Things to Come, by H. G. Wells. London and New York: The Macmillan Company, 1935, 155 pp.

345 *The Third Man*
London Films, 1949.
Directed by Carol Reed.
Original screenplay by Graham Greene.
The Third Man, by Graham Greene. London: Lorrimer Publishing, 1968, 134 pp. New York: Simon and Schuster, 1968, 134 pp.
The Cinema 1952, edited by Roger Manvell and R. K. Neilson Baxter. Harmondsworth, Middlesex: Penguin Books, 1952, pp. 68–87 (excerpt).
Teaching About the Film, by J. M. L. Peters. New York: International Documents Service (Columbia University Press), 1961, pp. 40–44 (excerpt).

346 *Thirty Seconds Over Tokyo*
Metro-Goldwyn-Mayer, 1944.
Directed by Mervyn LeRoy.
Screenplay by Dalton Trumbo.
Based on the book by Captain Ted W. Lawson and Robert Considine.
Best Film Plays—1945, edited by John Gassner and Dudley Nichols. New York: Crown Publishers, 1946, pp. 427–520.

347   *This Land Is Mine*
RKO Radio, 1943.
Directed by Jean Renoir.
Original screenplay by Dudley Nichols.
Twenty Best Film Plays, edited by John Gassner and Dudley
    Nichols. New York: Crown Publishers, 1943, pp. 833–874.

348   *Three Children*
Powers/Universal, 1913 (short).
Directed by Harry A. Pollard.
Original scenario by James Dayton.
The Motion Picture Story, by William Lord Wright. Chicago:
    Cloud Publishing Company, 1914, pp. 126–140.

349   *Through a Glass Darkly* (*Såsom i en Spegel*)
Svensk Filmindustri, 1961.
Directed by Ingmar Bergman.
Original screenplay by Ingmar Bergman.
A Film Trilogy, by Ingmar Bergman. New York: The Orion
    Press, 1967, pp. 13–61. London: Calder and Boyars, 1967,
    pp. 13–61.
Three Films by Ingmar Bergman. New York: Grove Press,
    1970, pp. 13–61.

350   *Through the Drifts*
Lubin, 19?? (short).
Original scenario by Lawrence S. McCloskey.
Scenario Writing, by Ernest N. Ross. Philadelphia: Penn
    Association, 1912, pp. 70–79.

351   *To Kill a Mockingbird*
Pakula-Mulligan–Brentwood–Universal-International, 1962.
Directed by Robert Mulligan.
Screenplay by Horton Foote.
Based on the novel by Harper Lee.
The Screenplay of To Kill a Mockingbird, by Horton Foote.
    New York: Harcourt, Brace & World, 1964, 117 pp.

352   *Tom Jones*
Woodfall, 1963.
Directed by Tony Richardson.
Screenplay by John Osborne.
Based on the novel by Henry Fielding.
Tom Jones, by John Osborne. London: Faber and Faber, 1964,
    142 pp. New York: Grove Press, 1964, 192 pp.
The Moving Image, by Robert Gessner. New York: E. P. Dutton
    & Co., 1968, pp. 41, 191–193 (excerpts).

353   *Transatlantic Merry-Go-Round*
Reliance/United Artists, 1934.
Directed by Benjamin Stoloff.
Original screenplay by Leon Gordon.
Additional scenes and dialogue by Joseph Moncure March
    and Harry W. Conn.
The New Technique of Screen Writing, by Tamar Lane.
    New York: Whittlesey House, 1936, pp. 209–331.

354   *A Tree Grows in Brooklyn*
Twentieth Century-Fox, 1945.
Directed by Elia Kazan.
Screenplay by Tess Slesinger and Frank Davis.

(Contributor to dialogue: Anita Loos.)
Based on the novel by Betty Smith.

Best Film Plays—1945, edited by John Gassner and Dudley
Nichols. New York: Crown Publishers, 1946, pp. 175–260.

355 *Trilogy*
Frank Perry/Allied Artists, 1969.
Part I: "Miriam."
Part II: "Among the Paths to Eden."
Part III: "A Christmas Memory."
Directed by Frank Perry.
Screenplays by Truman Capote and Eleanor Perry.
Based on the stories by Truman Capote.

Trilogy, by Truman Capote, Eleanor Perry and Frank Perry.
New York: The Macmillan Company, 1969, 276 pp.

356 *Trio*
Gainsborough, 1950.
Part I: "The Verger." Directed by Ken Annakin. Screenplay
by W. Somerset Maugham.
Part II: "Mr. Know-All." Directed by Ken Annakin.
Screenplay by R. C. Sherriff.
Part III: "Sanatorium." Directed by Harold French.
Screenplay by Noel Langley.
Based on the stories by W. Somerset Maugham.

Trio, by W. Somerset Maugham. Garden City: Doubleday
& Company, 1950, 156 pp.

357 *Tuesday*
Motion Picture Workshop, New York University, 1960 (short).
Instructor: Leo Hurwitz.

The Film-Maker's Art, by Haig P. Manoogian. New York: Basic Books, 1966, pp. 278–311.

358   *Twenty Years A-Growing*
Unproduced.
Screenplay (unfinished) by Dylan Thomas.
Based on the book by Maurice O'Sullivan.
Twenty Years A-Growing, by Dylan Thomas. London: J. M. Dent & Sons, 1964, 91 pp.
The Doctor and the Devils and Other Scripts, by Dylan Thomas. New York: New Directions, 1966, pp. 141–203.

359   *Two for the Road*
Twentieth Century-Fox, 1967.
Directed by Stanley Donen.
Original screenplay by Frederic Raphael.
Two for the Road, by Frederic Raphael. New York: Holt, Rinehart and Winston, 1967, 142 pp.

360   *2001: A Space Odyssey*
Metro-Goldwyn-Mayer, 1968.
Directed by Stanley Kubrick.
Screenplay by Stanley Kubrick and Arthur C. Clarke.
Based on the story "The Sentinel" by Arthur C. Clarke.
The Making of Kubrick's 2001, edited by Jerome Agel. New York: New American Library (Signet Books), 1970, pp. 292–294 (excerpts).

361   *Vectors*
Caravel Films/U. S. Navy, 1947 (documentary short).
Script by C. J. Wickwire.
Hollywood Quarterly, III, No. 1 (Fall 1947), 15–25.

362 *The Very Idea*
RKO Radio, 1929.
Directed by Richard Rosson and Frank Craven.
Screenplay by William LeBaron, based on his story.
Writing the Sound and Dialogue Photoplay, by Tom Terriss.
Hollywood: Palmer Institute of Authorship, 1930,
pp. 42-S–69-S (excerpts).

363 *Vinland the Good*
Unproduced.
Original screenplay by Nevil Shute.
Vinland the Good, by Nevil Shute. London: William Heinemann,
1946, 143 pp. New York: William Morrow & Co., 1946,
126 pp.

364 *The Virgin Spring* (*Jungfrukällan*)
Svensk Filmindustri, 1960.
Directed by Ingmar Bergman.
Screenplay by Ulla Isaksson.
Based on the medieval Swedish folk-song "The Daughter of
Töre of Vänge."
The Virgin Spring, by Ulla Isaksson. New York: Ballantine
Books, 1961, 114 pp.

365 *Viridiana*
Gustavo Alatriste, 1961.
Directed by Luis Buñuel.
Screenplay by Luis Buñuel and Julio Alejandro.
Based on an original story by Luis Buñuel.
Three Screen Plays, by Luis Buñuel. New York: The Orion
Press, 1969, pp. 1–109.

Luis Buñuel, by Ado Kyrou. New York: Simon and Schuster, 1963, pp. 164–177 (excerpts).
Elements of Film, by Lee R. Bobker. New York: Harcourt, Brace & World, 1969, pp. 32-42 (excerpt).

366   *I Vitelloni*
Peg Film-Cité Films, 1953.
Directed by Federico Fellini.
Screenplay by Federico Fellini, Ennio Flaiano and Tullio Pinelli.
Based on an original story by Federico Fellini and Ennio Flaiano.
Three Screenplays, by Federico Fellini. New York: The Orion Press, 1970, pp. 1–132.

367   *The War Game*
B. B. C., 1966.
Directed by Peter Watkins.
Original screenplay by Peter Watkins.
The War Game, by Peter Watkins. London: Sphere Books and Andre Deutsch, 1967, 128 pp. New York: Avon Books, 1967, 128 pp.

368   *Watch on the Rhine*
Warner Bros., 1943.
Directed by Herman Shumlin.
Screenplay by Dashiell Hammett.
Additional scenes and dialogue by Lillian Hellman.
Based on the play by Lillian Hellman.
Best Film Plays of 1943–1944, edited by John Gassner and Dudley Nichols. New York: Crown Publishers, 1945, pp. 299–356.

369   *Wells Fargo*
Paramount, 1937.
Directed by Frank Lloyd.
Screenplay by Paul Schofield, Gerald Geraghty and
   Frederick Jackson.
(Contributor to screenplay construction: Howard Estabrook.
   Contributors to dialogue: Eddie Welch, Duke Atteberry and
   Howard Estabrook.)
Based on an unpublished story by Stuart N. Lake.
Foremost Films of 1938, by Frank Vreeland. New York and
   Chicago: Pitman Publishing Corporation, 1939, pp.
   33–48 (excerpts).

370   *White Nights* (*Le Notti Bianche*)
Vides, 1957.
Directed by Luchino Visconti.
Screenplay by Suso Cecchi d'Amico and Luchino Visconti.
Based on the story by Feodor Dostoevski.
Three Screenplays, by Luchino Visconti. New York: The Orion
   Press, 1970, pp. 1–91.

371   *Whose Little Baby Are You?*
Universal, 1921 (short).
Directed by William H. Watson.
Original scenario by W. Scott Darling.
Photoplay Writing, by William Lord Wright. New York: Falk
   Publishing Co., 1922, pp. 133–144 (excerpt).

372   *The Wild Party*
Paramount, 1929.
Directed by Dorothy Arzner.
Screenplay by E. Lloyd Sheldon.

Dialogue by John V. A. Weaver.

Based on the novel *Unforbidden Fruit* by Warner Fabian.

Writing the Sound and Dialogue Photoplay, by Tom Terriss. Hollywood: Palmer Institute of Authorship, 1930, pp. 70-S–108-S (excerpts).

373 *Wild Strawberries (Smultronstället)*
Svensk Filmindustri, 1957.
Directed by Ingmar Bergman.
Original screenplay by Ingmar Bergman.
Four Screenplays of Ingmar Bergman. New York: Simon and Schuster, 1960, pp. 165–239.

374 *Wilson*
Twentieth Century-Fox, 1944.
Directed by Henry King.
Original screenplay by Lamar Trotti.
Best Film Plays of 1943–1944, edited by John Gassner and Dudley Nichols. New York: Crown Publishers, 1945, pp. 7–87.

375 *Wind Across the Everglades*
Schulberg/Warner Bros., 1958.
Directed by Nicholas Ray.
Original screenplay by Budd Schulberg.
Across the Everglades, by Budd Schulberg. New York: Random House, 1958, 126 pp. New York: Bantam Books, 1958, 151 pp.

376 *Winners of the West*
Universal, 1921 (serial).
Directed by Edward Laemmle.
Original scenario by Ford Beebe and Robert Dillon .

Photoplay Writing, by William Lord Wright. New York: Falk
  Publishing Co., 1922, pp. 115–124 (excerpts).

377   *Winter Light* (*The Communicants*) (*Nattvardsgästerna*)
Svensk Filmindustri, 1963.
Directed by Ingmar Bergman.
Original screenplay by Ingmar Bergman.
A Film Trilogy, by Ingmar Bergman. New York: The Orion
  Press, 1967, pp. 63–104. London: Calder and Boyars, 1967,
  pp. 63–104.
Three Films by Ingmar Bergman. New York: Grove Press,
  1970, pp. 63–104.

378   *Witchcraft*
Jesse L. Lasky/Paramount, 1916.
Directed by Frank Reicher.
Scenario by Margaret Turnbull.
Based on the story "Humility o' Hedford" by R. Ralston Reed.
Cinema Craftsmanship, by Frances Taylor Patterson. New
  York: Harcourt, Brace and Company, 1921, Second Edition,
  pp. 200–266.

379   *Without Reward*
Nestor, 1913 (short).
Original scenario by Arthur Leeds.
Writing the Photoplay, by J. Berg Esenwein and Arthur Leeds.
  Springfield, Mass.: The Home Correspondence School,
  1913, pp. 331–351.

380   *Woman in the Dunes* (*Suna no Onna*)
Teshigahara Productions, 1964.

Directed by Hiroshi Teshigahara.
Screenplay by Kobo Abe, based on his novel.
Woman in the Dunes, by Hiroshi Teshigahara. New York:
Phaedra Publishers, 1966, 94 pp.

381   *The Women*
Metro-Goldwyn-Mayer, 1939.
Directed by George Cukor.
Screenplay by Anita Loos and Jane Murfin.
Based on the play by Clare Boothe.
Twenty Best Film Plays, edited by John Gassner and Dudley
Nichols. New York: Crown Publishers, 1943, pp. 61–130.

382   *Wonder Man*
Samuel Goldwyn/RKO Radio, 1945.
Directed by Bruce Humberstone.
Screenplay by Don Hartman, Melville Shavelson and Philip
Rapp.
Adaptation by Jack Jevne and E. Edwin Moran.
Based on an original story by Arthur Sheekman.
The Screen Writer, I, No. 3 (August 1945), 14–22 (excerpts).

383   *Wuthering Heights*
Samuel Goldwyn/United Artists, 1939.
Directed by William Wyler.
Screenplay by Ben Hecht and Charles MacArthur.
Based on the novel by Emily Brontë.
Twenty Best Film Plays, edited by John Gassner and Dudley
Nichols. New York: Crown Publishers, 1943, pp. 293–331.
The Moving Image, by Robert Gessner. New York: E. P.
Dutton & Co., 1968, pp. 171–179 (excerpts).

384   *Yellow Jack*
Metro-Goldwyn-Mayer, 1938.
Directed by George B. Seitz.
Screenplay by Edward Chodorov.
(Contributor to treatment: Dan Totheroh.)
Based on the play by Sidney Howard in collaboration with Paul
   de Kruif.
Twenty Best Film Plays, edited by John Gassner and Dudley
   Nichols. New York: Crown Publishers, 1943, pp. 1039–1080.

385   *You Can't Take It With You*
Columbia, 1938.
Directed by Frank Capra.
Screenplay by Robert Riskin.
Based on the play by George S. Kaufman and Moss Hart.
Foremost Films of 1938, by Frank Vreeland. New York and
   Chicago: Pitman Publishing Corporation, 1939, pp. 129–146
   (excerpts).

386   *The Young in Heart*
Selznick International/United Artists, 1938.
Directed by Richard Wallace.
Screenplay by Paul Osborn.
Adaptation by Charles Bennett.
Based on the novel *The Gay Banditti* by I. A. R. Wylie.
Foremost Films of 1938, by Frank Vreeland. New York and
   Chicago: Pitman Publishing Corporation, 1939, pp. 164–181
   (excerpts).

387   *The Young Savages*
Contemporary Productions/United Artists, 1961.
Directed by John Frankenheimer.

Screenplay by Edward Anhalt and J. P. Miller.
Based on the novel *A Matter of Conviction* by Evan Hunter.
The Cinema of John Frankenheimer, by Gerald Pratley.
London: A. Zwemmer, 1969, pp. 52–53 (excerpt). New
York: A. S. Barnes & Co., 1969, pp. 52–53 (excerpt).

388   *Youth's Endearing Charm*
American/Mutual, 1916.
Directed by William Dowlan.
Original scenario by Maibelle Heikes Justice.
How to Write for the "Movies," by Louella O. Parsons.
Chicago: A. C. McClurg & Co., 1917, pp. 142–236.

Index

A-B-C of Motion Pictures, 1
Abbott, George, 10, 56
Abe, Kobo, 380
Across the Everglades, 375
Adams, Samuel Hopkins, 179
Agadzhanova-Shutko, Nina, 35
Agee, James, 5, 12, 50, 53, 160, 229, 250, 254
Agee on Film, Volume Two, 5, 50, 53, 250, 254
Agel, Jerome, 360
Akutagawa, Ryunosuke, 267, 288
Alcoriza, Luis, 105
Alcott, Louisa May, 211
Alejandro, Julio, 248, 318, 365
Alexander, Donald, 97
Alexandrov, Grigori, 15, 262, 287, 333, 335
Alianello, Carlo, 308
"Alien Corn, The," 286
Alison, Joan, 66
Ambler, Eric, 102
American Tragedy, An, 15, 276
Amidei, Sergio, 270
"Among Lonely Women," 17
"Among the Paths to Eden," 355
Andalusian Dog, An, 72
Anderson, Lindsay, 167, 307
Anderson, Maxwell, 10, 184
Andrews, Del, 10, 189

Angel Exterminador, El, 105
Angel Street, 125
Anhalt, Edward, 387
Annakin, Ken, 57, 286, 356
Année Dernière à Marienbad, L', 201
Anouilh, Jean, 20
Ansiktet, 220
"Ant and the Grasshopper, The," 102
Antonioni, 17
Antonioni, Michelangelo, 17, 26, 99, 144, 258
April Romance, 48
Apuleius, 109
Art of Photoplay Writing, The (Carr), 174
Art of Photo-Play Writing, The (Weston), 310
Art of the Film, The, 125
Art of the Photoplay, The, 70, 216
Artaud, Antonin, 313
Arzner, Dorothy, 372
Asano, 18
Ashelbe, Detective, 8
Asquith, Anthony, 171, 284
Atkins, Tommy, 317
Atlas, Leopold, 124
Atteberry, Duke, 369

"Au Bord du Lit," 185
Audiberti, Jacques, 65
Audiovisual Script Writing, 23, 261
Axelrod, George, 226

"Babylon Revisited," 80
Balchin, Nigel, 236
Ball, Eustace Hale, 70, 157, 186, 216
Band, Albert, 291
Barillet, Pierre, 39
Barrie, James M., 197, 272
Bartolini, Elio, 26, 99, 144
Bartolini, Luigi, 42
"Basement Room, The," 108
Bassani, Giorgio, 308
Baxter, R. K. Neilson, 69, 139, 194, 202, 307, 345
Beauties of the Night, 39
Beauty and the Devil, 38
Beck, Reginald, 153
Beckett, Samuel, 113
Beebe, Ford, 376
Beeding, Francis, 324
Behrman, S. N., 19
Bell, Mary Hayley, 305
Bellocchio, Marco, 74
Benét, Stephen Vincent, 11
Bennett, Charles, 386
Beranger, Clara, 337
Bergamin, José, 105
Bergman, Helmer W., 52
Bergman, Ingmar, 220, 309, 315, 319, 349, 364, 373, 377
Bernds, Edward 285
Berto, Giusèppe, 33
Best Film Plays—1945, 94, 124, 212, 232, 255, 268, 322, 324, 346, 354
Best Film Plays of 1943–1944, 66, 95, 130, 146, 238, 242, 269, 283, 368, 374

Best Pictures, 1939–1940, The, 29, 86, 90, 134, 240, 253, 289
Betts, Ernest, 183, 280
Biancoli, Oreste, 42
Biberman, Herbert J., 301
Bigelow, Ernest N., 337
Biro, Lajos, 200, 280
Blank, Dorothy Ann, 320
Blankfort, Michael, 62
Blaue Engel, Der, 49
Blystone, John G., 266
Bob Dylan: Don't Look Back, 93
Bobker, Lee R., 129, 156, 201, 309, 365
Boccaccio '70, 185, 339
Boito, Camillo, 308
Boland, Bridget, 125
Bolt, Robert, 91
Bonicelli, Vittorio, 41
Booker, Bob, 271
Boothe, Clare, 381
Boulle, Pierre, 54
Bound and Gagged, 275
Bower, Dallas, 96
Bowles, Paul, 308
Box, Sydney, 32
Brackett, Charles, 212, 253, 334
Brackett, Leigh, 44
Bradbury, Ray, 107
Bradley, Willard King, 314
Brand, Christianna, 307
Brand, Max, 86
Branston, Brian, 2
Breaking Into the Movies, 292
Breffort, Alexandre, 177
Brenon, Herbert, 197, 323
Bretherton, Vivien R., 215
Bridge of Ghisolfa, The, 294
Bridge Over the River Kwai, The, 54
Bright, John, 31
Brontë, Emily, 383
Brooke, Van Dyke, 117

Brown, Clarence, 19, 164
Brown, Harry, 15, 276
Bruckman, Clyde, 266
Brulé, Claude, 204
Brunel, Adrian, 20, 57, 64, 170, 207
Buchanan, Andrew, 233
Buchman, Sidney, 154, 240, 268
Buck, Pearl S., 95, 133
Bucquet, Harold S., 95
Budgen, Suzanne, 331
Buñuel, Luis, 6, 72, 105, 248, 318, 365
Burford, Roger, 48
Burnett, Murray, 66
Burnett, W. R., 209
Burnside, Norman, 90
Busch, Niven, 172, 278
Buster Keaton, 266
Butler, Frank, 130, 232
Butler, Hugo, 322
Byrne, Richard B., 61, 132, 257

Cady, Jerome, 283
Cain, James M., 8, 94, 278
Caine, Clarence J., 168
California Quarterly, The, 301
Cameron, Ian, 17
Campanile, Pasquale Festa, 294
Cannon, Robert, 58
Capote, Truman, 37, 355
Capra, Frank, 179, 198, 240, 385
Carabinieri, I, 65
Carl Th. Dreyer, 182
Carné, Marcel, 73
Carpenter, Elizabeth R., 117
Carr, Catherine, 174
Cary, Joyce, 307
Caster, Paul, 261
Cavett, Frank, 130
Cayrol, Jean, 249
Cendrars, Blaise, 335
Cespedes, Alba de, 17

Chandler, Raymond, 44, 94
Chaplin, Charles, 131
Chayefsky, Paddy, 30, 129
Cheever, John, 336
Chiari, Mario, 237
Chodorov, Edward, 384
"Christmas Memory, A," 355
Cina e Vicina, La, 74
Cinema, 131
Cinema Craftsmanship, 378
Cinema 1952, The, 69, 139, 194, 202, 307, 345
Cinema of John Frankenheimer, The, 226, 387
Cinema of Orson Welles, The, 77, 221
Cinema Plays, 157, 186
Cinemages, 27, 85, 89, 160, 161, 293, 304
Clair, René, 38, 39, 127, 136, 316
Clansman, The, 45
Clark, Walter Van Tilburg, 269
Clarke, Arthur C., 360
Clarke, Douglas, 79
Clarke, T. E. B., 102, 202
Clarkson, Stephen, 84
Classic Film Collector, 213
Clemens, Samuel L., 4
Cluny, Geneviève, 110
Clutsam, G. H., 48
Cocteau, Jean, 47, 264, 341
Coffee, Lenore, 103
Collected Short Prose of James Agee, The, 160, 229
College Treasury, A, 286
Collet, Jean, 13, 65, 75, 110, 219
Collier, John W., 178
Collings, Pierre, 330
Collins, Richard, 172
"'Colonel's Lady, The," 286
Colpi, Henri, 25
Communicants, The, 377
Condon, Richard, 226

112

Confrontation des Meilleurs Films de Tous les Temps, 77
Conn, Harry W., 353
Connelly, Marc, 133
Connolly, Myles, 240
Considine, Robert, 346
Conway, Jack, 95
Copperfield '70, 82
Coquille et le Clergyman, La, 313
Cormack, Bartlett, 123
Cornelius, Henry, 178
Corso, Gregory, 271
Cosmological Eye, The, 304
Costello, Donald P., 22, 87, 284
Courteline, Georges, 136
Coward, Noel, 55
Cowie, Peter, 77, 221
Cox, Vivian, 32
Crabtree, Arthur, 286
Crane, Stephen, 50, 53, 291
Craven, Frank, 362
Creedon, Richard, 320
Crichton, Charles, 202
Crisp, Donald, 243
Cromwell, John, 8, 129
Cronin, A. J., 76
Crossman, Melville, 283
"Crusaders," 167
Cukor, George, 211, 295, 381
Cunningham, Jack, 297
Curry, George, 82
Curtiz, Michael, 66
Curwood, James Oliver, 116

Dali, Salvador, 6, 27, 72
Dalrymple, Ian, 76, 284
D'Amico, Suso Cecchi, 17, 42, 185, 237, 294, 308, 370
Dane, Clemence, 19
Darling, W. Scott, 371
"Daughter of Töre of Vänge, The," 364
Davis, Frank, 354

Dayton, James, 348
De Antonio, Emile, 277
Dearden, Basil, 64
Death Day, 287
Death in Seven Hours, 84
Death in the Family, A, 12
De Concini, Ennio, 144
De Kruif, Paul, 112, 384
De Laurot, Edouard, 128
DeLeon, Walter, 297
Delmar, Viña, 223
De Maris, Merrill, 320
DeMille, Cecil B., 59
D'Ennery, Adolphe, 323
Dent, Alan, 148, 153
De Sica, Vittorio, 42, 237
Det Sjunde Inseglet, 309
"Devil and Daniel Webster, The," 11
Diamond, I. A. L., 177, 321
Dickens, Charles, 82, 138, 139
Dickinson, Thorold, 125, 307
Dieterle, William, 11, 46, 90, 187, 206, 330
Dighton, John, 87, 194
Dillon, Robert, 376
Dix, Beulah Marie, 323
Dixon, Thomas, Jr., 45
Dmytryk, Edward, 62, 103
Doctor and the Devils and Other Scripts, The, 89, 358
Documentary News Letter, 265
Don César de Bazan, 323
Donen, Stanley, 359
Dostoevski, Feodor, 370
Dowlan, William, 388
Downey, Robert, 67
Doyle, Arthur Conan, 213
Dracula, 257
Drama in Our Time, 164
Dreiser, Theodore, 15, 276
Drew, Mrs. Sidney, 126
Dreyer, Carl Th., 182

Drinkwater, John, 48
Dulac, Germaine, 313
Dumanoir, 323
Du Maurier, Daphne, 289
Dunne, Philip, 163
Dunning, Philip, 56
Duras, Marguerite, 25, 156
Duvivier, Julien, 20
Dylan, Bob, 93
Dyssegaard, Søren, 182

Eastman, Charles, 210
Eastman, Phil, 58
Eclipse, The, 99
Edison Catalogue, 142, 205
Edwards, Walter, 302
Eisenstein, Sergei M., 7, 15, 35,
111, 180, 262, 287, 333, 335
*Elbert Moore's Text Book on
Writing the Photoplay,* 71
Eldridge, John, 265
Elements of Film, 129, 156, 201,
309, 365
*Elinor Glyn System of Writing,
The,* 141
Eliot, T. S., 245
Emergence of Film Art, The, 142,
205
Emerson, John, 214, 292
Endore, Guy, 124
Enfants du Paradis, Les, 73
Englander, Otto, 320
Engrenage, L', 173
Epstein, Julius J., 66
Epstein, Philip G., 66
Esenwein, J. Berg, 379
Estabrook, Howard, 164, 369
Everybody Comes to Rick's, 66
Experimental Cinema, 10, 287

Fabbri, Dieggo, 33
Fabian, Warner, 372
Face to Face, 53

"Facts of Life, The," 286
Fainlight, Harry, 149
Fairfax, Marion, 213
Faragoh, Francis Edwards, 209
Farnum, Dorothy, 183
Farquharson, J., 306
Fast, Howard, 155
Faulkner, William, 44
Faust, Frederick, 86
Feature Photoplay, The, 126, 193,
263
Federico Fellini, 43, 92, 100, 252,
331
Fejos, Paul, 56
Fellini, 331
Fellini, Federico, 43, 92, 100, 109,
191, 252, 270, 331, 339, 366
Femme Mariée, La, 230
Ferber, Edna, 126
Feuchtwanger, Lion, 183
Fielding, Henry, 352
Fifty Years of Peter Pan, 272
Film: Book 1, 254
Film: Book 2, 203, 249
Film Culture, 101, 128, 149, 196,
270
Film in the Making, A, 178
Film-Maker's Art, The, 357
Film Maker's Guide, A, 2
*Film of Murder in the Cathedral,
The,* 245
Film Script, 20, 57, 64
Film Sense, The, 15, 111, 333,
335
Film Trilogy, A, 315, 349, 377
Film Writing Forms, 104, 262
Filmcraft, 170, 207
Films, 85, 229
Films and Filming, 294
Films of Tyranny, 61, 132, 257
Films: The Way of the Cinema,
233
"Finest Tradition, The," 23

114

Fitzgerald, F. Scott, 80
Flaiano, Ennio, 43, 92, 100, 191, 252, 258, 331, 339, 366
"Flames on the Horizon," 23
Fleischer, Richard, 33
Fleming, Victor, 184, 292
Flournoy, Richard, 242
Fonda, Peter, 98
Foote, Horton, 351
Ford, John, 137, 163, 175, 327
Foreman, Carl, 68
Foremost Films of 1938, 8, 59, 76, 172, 215, 320, 342, 369, 385, 386
Forester, C. S., 5
Foster, George, 271
Foster, Lewis R., 240, 242
Four Screenplays (Clair), 38, 39, 136, 316
Four Screenplays of Ingmar Bergman, 220, 309, 319, 373
Four-Star Scripts, 179, 198, 211, 330
Fowler, Gene, 235
Franci, Adolfo, 42, 237
Franciosa, Massimo, 294
Frank, Robert, 282
Frankenheimer, John, 226, 387
Franklin, Sidney, 133
French, Harold, 102, 286, 356
Frend, Charles, 305
Friedman, Bruce Jay, 271
Froeschel, George, 241
From Script to Screen, 236
"Frontier Films' Production No. 5," 247
Fry, Christopher, 33, 41
Furie, Sidney J., 210
Furthman, Charles, 56
Furthman, Jules, 44, 133, 312

Galeen, Henrik, 132, 257
Gance, Abel, 196

Garnett, Tay, 278
Gassner, John, 11, 66, 94, 95, 112, 123, 124, 130, 133, 137, 146, 154, 163, 179, 187, 206, 209, 212, 223, 232, 238, 240, 241, 242, 246, 255, 268, 269, 283, 289, 322, 324, 327, 346, 347 354, 368, 374, 381, 383, 384
Gay Banditti, The, 386
"General, The," 200
General Line, The, 262
Geraghty, Gerald, 369
Géronimi, Jérôme, 136
Gessner, Robert, 4, 7, 9, 19, 37, 44, 54, 62, 68, 77, 80, 103, 107, 122, 138, 139, 143, 148, 152, 153, 171, 175, 180, 204, 220, 227, 251, 260, 269, 276, 278, 280, 284, 285, 291, 297, 309, 328, 332, 334, 352, 383
Gherardi, Gherardo, 42
Gibney, Sheridan, 330
"Gigolo and Gigolette," 102
Gilson, René, 47, 264, 341
Ginsberg, Allen, 271
Ginsberg, Milton Moses, 78
Girl Friends, The, 17
Giulietta degli Spiriti, 191
Glyn, Elinor, 141
Godard, Jean-Luc, 13, 65, 75, 110, 219, 230, 231, 273, 274
Goetz, Ruth and Augustus, 152
Gold, Herbert, 271
Goldbeck, Willis, 197
Golden Age, The, 6
Golden Ass, The, 109
Goldman, James, 208
Goldman, William, 60
Goodrich, John F., 200
Gordon, Leon, 353
Gordon, Ruth, 268
Gorky, Maxim, 85
Grand Maneuver, The, 136

Grande Illusion, La, 135
Grandon, F. J., 168
Great Film Plays, 11, 133, 179, 206, 289, 327
Grédy, Jean-Pierre, 39
Green, F. L., 259
Green, Roger Lancelyn, 272
Greene, Graham, 103, 108, 299, 345
Greenwood, Walter, 69
Gregory, Horace, 160
Griffin, Jonathan, 41
Griffith, D. W., 45, 176
Grimm, Brothers, 320
Gruault, Jean, 65, 190
Grubb, Davis, 250
Guerra, Tonino, 26, 99, 258
Guerrieri, Gerardo, 42

Hall, Alexander, 154
Hamer, Robert, 178, 194
Hamilton, Patrick, 125
Hammett, Dashiell, 368
Hand, David, 320
Hanemann, H. W., 317
Harbou, Thea von, 218
Harding, Bertita, 187
Hardy, Thomas, 96
Harrison, Joan, 289
Harrison, Louis Reeves, 40
Harrison, Richard, 84
Hart, Moss, 385
Hartman, Don, 382
Harvey, Anthony, 208
Hashimoto, Shinobu, 169, 288
Hatch, Eric, 246
Hatcher, Harlan, 175
Havelock-Allan, Anthony, 55, 139
Havez, Jean, 266
Hawks, Howard, 44
Hawthorne, Nathaniel, 303
Haycox, Ernest, 327
Hayes, Alfred, 42, 270

Heaven Can Wait, 154
Hecht, Ben, 324, 383
Heerman, Victor, 211
Hellman, Lillian, 256, 368
Helvick, James, 37
Henley, Hobart, 126
Henry, O., 338
Herald, Heinz, 90, 206
Herbert, F. Hugh, 342
Herczeg, Geza, 206
Here Is Your War, 124
Hervey, Harry, 312
Hevener, J. T., 158
High Explosive, 170
Hill, Elizabeth, 76
Hill, George Roy, 60
Hilton, James, 134, 241
Hitchcock, Alfred, 289, 324
Hoellering, George, 245
Hoffenstein, Samuel, 15
Hogan, Michael, 289
Hold Autumn in Your Hand, 322
Hollywood Quarterly, 58, 83, 148, 361
Holt, Paul, 32
Honnête Homme, Un, 159
Hopper, Dennis, 98
Horace, 109
Horniman, Roy, 194
House of Dr. Edwardes, The, 324
House of Incest, The, 304
How to Write a Photoplay, 114, 115, 117, 243, 325
How to Write and Sell Film Stories, 3
How to Write Commentaries for Films, 79
How to Write Film Stories for Amateur Films, 84
How to Write for the "Movies," 158, 388
How to Write Photoplays, 168, 214

Howard, Leslie, 284
Howard, Sidney, 384
Howard, William K., 31
Howlett, John, 167
Hoyt, Harry O., 213
Hubley, John, 58
Huff, Theodore, 45, 176
Hughes, Robert, 203, 249, 254
Hulfish, David Sherill, 234
Humberstone, Bruce, 382
"Humility o' Hedford," 378
Hunter, Evan, 387
Hurd, Earl, 320
Hurwitz, Leo, 247, 357
Huston, John, 5, 37, 41, 90, 187, 203, 239, 251, 291

Ibsen, Henrik, 104
"In the Grove," 267, 288
Ince, Thomas H., 302
Information Film, The, 296
Inge, William, 326
Inside Secrets of Photoplay Writing, 314
Isaksson, Ulla, 364
Israel Rank, 194
Ivory, James, 162

Jackson, Charles, 212
Jackson, Felix, 29, 86
Jackson, Frederick, 369
Jackson, Pat, 102
Jacobs, Lewis, 45, 104, 142, 176, 205, 262
Jacobson, Egon, 218
Jag Ar Nyfiken—Blaa, 165
Jag Ar Nyfiken—Gul, 166
James, Benedict, 306
James, Henry, 152
James, Polly, 285
Janowitz, Hans, 61
Jarlot, Gérard, 25
Jean Cocteau, 47, 264, 341

Jean-Luc Godard, 13, 65, 75, 110, 219
Jennings, Talbot, 133, 295
Jevne, Jack, 382
Jhabvala, Ruth Prawer, 162
Jirásek, Alois, 181
Joan of Lorraine, 184
John, Errol, 88, 118, 150
John Huss, 181
Johnson, Arthur, 121
Johnson, Nunnally, 137
Jones, Grover, 59
Jones, James, 122
Jones, Lon, 33
Joppolo, Benjamino, 65
Jordan, Mildred R., 311
Jordan, William E., 311
Jorgensen, Paul A., 286
Josef von Sternberg, 18, 312
Josephson, Matthew, 206
Juarez and Maximilian, 187
Jugger, The, 219
Jules et Jim, 190
Jungfrukällen, 364
Justice, Maibelle Heikes, 140, 388

Kabinett des Doktor Caligari, Das, 61
Kanin, Fay, 267
Kanin, Garson, 29
Kanin, Michael, 267
Kaplan, Nelly, 196
Katterjohn, Monte M., 141
Kaufman, Charles, 203
Kaufman, George S., 385
Kazan, Elia, 14, 28, 106, 326, 332, 354
Kearney, Patrick, 276
Keaton, Buster, 266
Keene, Ralph, 81
Keon, Barbara, 4
Keown, Eric, 127
Kerouac, Jack, 282

Kerr, Geoffrey, 127
Kibbee, Roland, 87
Kimmins, Anthony, 236
King, Carlton, 193
King, Henry, 172, 374
Kirkland, David, 214
Kirkland, Jack, 335
Kirsch, Maurice, 79
Kirwan, Patrick, 64
Kitchin, Laurence, 32
"Kite, The," 286
Kline, Herbert, 119
Klinger, Werner, 10
Klumph, Inez and Helen, 116
Koch, Howard, 66
Kopit, Arthur, 271
Korda, Alexander, 280
Kramer, Stanley, 188
Krasna, Norman, 29, 123
Kratochvíl, Miloš V., 181
Kravchunovsky, I., 333
Kubrick, Stanley, 360
Kurosawa, Akira, 169, 267, 288
Kyrou, Ado, 6, 72, 159, 248, 365

La Barthe, Henri, 8
La Bern, Arthur J., 178
La Cava, Gregory, 246
Laclos, Choderlos de, 204
Ladri di Biciclette, 42
Laemmle, Edward, 63, 376
Lafitte the Pirate, 59
Lagerkvist, Pär, 33
Lahue, Kalton C., 275
Lait, Jack, 263
Lake, Stuart N., 369
Lamb, Harold, 59
Lane, Tamar, 353
Lang, Fritz, 123, 218
Lang, Walter, 235
Langley, Noel, 356
Lardner, Ring, 68
Lardner, Ring, Jr., 58

Lathrop, William Addison, 151
Lattuada, Alberto, 227
Laughton, Charles, 250
Laurence, Dale, 207
Lavoro, Il, 185
Lawrence, Josephine, 223
Lawson, John Howard, 8, 46
Lawson, Ted W., 346
Lean, David, 54, 55, 91, 139
Leary, Helen and Nolan, 223
LeBaron, William, 362
Lee, Harper, 351
Lee, Laurie, 81
Lee, Norman, 48, 138
Leeds, Arthur, 379
Legg, Stuart, 270
Lengyel, Melchior, 253
Leprohon, Pierre, 17, 144, 258
Lerner, Irving, 83
LeRoy, Mervyn, 209, 346
Le Saint, E. J., 151
Leslie, Alfred, 282
Levien, Sonya, 172
Lewis, Cecil, 284
Lewis, Sinclair, 329
Liebmann, Robert, 49
Lindgren, Ernest, 125
Linich, Billy, 149
Lipscomb, W. P., 284
Little Soldier, The, 273
Little Stories from the Screen, 151
Lives of the Ceasars, 109
Living Screen, The, 199
Llewellyn, Richard, 163, 255
Lloyd, Frank, 369
Logan, M., 321
Loos, Anita, 176, 214, 292, 354, 381
Lorentz, Pare, 112
Love Burglar, The, 263
Lowe, Edward T., Jr., 56
Lower Depths, The, 85
Lubitsch, Ernst, 253

Lubitsch Touch, The, 253
Ludwig, Edward, 342
Ludwig, William, 215
Luis Buñuel, 6, 72, 248, 365
Lyons, Timothy J., 131
Lytton, Grace, 338

MacArthur, Charles, 383
Macaulay, Richard, 29, 86, 90, 134, 240, 253, 289
Macdonald, David, 32
MacDonald, Philip, 289
Machiavelli, Niccolò, 227
Mackendrick, Alexander, 199
MacKenzie, Aeneas, 187
MacPhail, Angus, 64, 178, 207, 233, 324
Macpherson, Jeanie, 59
MacRae, Arthur, 102, 297
"Madame La Gimp," 198
Maddow, Ben, 83
Magni, Luigi, 227
Making a Film, 307
Making of Kubrick's 2001, The, 360
Malraux, André, 229
Man About Town, 316
Mandrake, The, 227
Mankiewicz, Herman J., 77, 200
Mankiewicz, Joseph L., 9, 192
Mann, Abby, 188
Mann, Delbert, 30, 82
Mann, Heinrich, 49
Mann, Klauss, 270
Manning, Bruce, 342
Manoogian, Haig P., 357
Manvell, Roger, 55, 69, 139, 194, 199, 202, 259, 305, 307, 345
Manwaring, Elizabeth W., 16
March, Joseph Moncure, 353
March of Time, The, 16, 244
Margrave, Seton, 127
Marion, Frances, 3, 133, 303

Marsan, Jean, 136
Marshall, George, 86
Marshman, D. M., Jr., 334
Martin, Townsend, 197
Maruyama, Michiro, 18
Maschwitz, Eric, 134
Masculin-Féminin, 231
Mason, Sarah Y., 211
Mathis, June, 323
Matter of Conviction, A, 387
Matter of Life and Death, A, 328
Maugham, W. Somerset, 102, 286, 356
Maupassant, Guy de, 185, 231
Mayer, Carl, 61
Mayer, Edwin Justus, 59
Mayo, Archie, 3
Mayorga, Margaret, 97, 244
Maysles, Albert and David, 300
McCardell, Roy L., 71
McCarey, Leo, 130, 223, 297
McCloskey, Lawrence S., 24, 121, 350
McCoy, Horace, 343
McGivern, Cecil, 139
McNutt, William Slavens, 297
McTeague, 143
Meade, Walter, 305
Medioli, Enrico, 294
Mendes, Lothar, 183, 225
Menzies, William Cameron, 344
Meredyth, Bess, 235
Metamorphoses, 109
Meyrink, Gustav, 132
Michel, André, 249
Michelangelo Antonioni, 17, 144, 258
Middleton, Ethel Styles, 189
Miles, Bernard, 69
Milestone, Lewis, 10, 256, 260, 283
Miller, Arthur, 239
Miller, Henry, 304

Miller, J. P., 387
Miller, Seton I., 154
Milne, A. A., 233
Minkin, Adolf, 281
Miracolo a Milano, 237
"Miriam," 355
"Mr. Know-All," 356
Mitchell, Joseph, 266
Modern British Dramas, 175
Modern Dramas, 175
Moineaux, Georges, 136
Molinaro, Ursule, 230
Money for Film Stories, 48, 138
Montagu, Ivor, 15, 305, 335
Moore, Elbert, 71
Moore, Stephen, 31, 247
Moran, E. Edwin, 382
Morgan, George, 63
Morgan, Guy, 20, 64
Mosel, Tad, 12
Motion Picture Continuities, 197, 200, 303
Motion Picture Story, The, 21, 140, 348
Motion Picture Work, 234
Moussinac, Léon, 7, 35, 287
Moussy, Marcel, 120
Moving Image, The, 4, 7, 9, 19, 37, 44, 54, 62, 68, 77, 80, 103, 107, 122, 138, 139, 143, 148, 152, 153, 171, 175, 180, 204, 220, 227, 251, 260, 269, 276, 278, 280, 284, 285, 291, 297, 309, 328, 332, 334, 352, 383
Mulligan, Robert, 351
Murfin, Jane, 95, 381
Murnau, F. W., 257
Myers, Henry, 86
Myton, Fred, 224

Nagelberg, M. M., 164
Nattvardsgästerna, 377
Neame, Ronald, 55, 139

Neilan, Marshall, 4
Nelson, J. Arthur, 217
New Fields for the Writer, 31, 247
New Letters in America, 160
New Technique of Screen Writing, The, 353
Nichols, Dudley, 11, 66, 94, 95, 112, 123, 124, 130, 133, 137, 146, 154, 163, 175, 179, 187, 206, 209, 212, 223, 232, 238, 240, 241, 242, 246, 255, 268, 269, 283, 289, 322, 324, 327, 346, 347, 354, 368, 374, 381, 383, 384
Night, The, 258
"Night Bus," 179
Nin, Anaïs, 161, 304
Noble, Lorraine, 179, 198, 211, 330
Norris, Frank, 143
North, Wilfred, 71
Notti Bianche, Le, 370
Notti di Cabiria, Le, 252
Nuit et Brouillard, 249

O'Brien, Willis H., 213
Obsession, 274
Odets, Clifford, 255
O'Donnell, Jack, 317
Of the People, 16
O'Flaherty, Liam, 175
Oguni, Hideo, 169
Olivier, Laurence, 148, 153, 279
On Picture-Play Writing: A Handbook of Workmanship, 228
One Act Play Magazine, 31, 46, 281
"One Is Guilty," 84
One-Reel Scenarios for Amateur Movie-Makers, 97, 244
O'Neil, Barry, 24

O'Neil, George, 335
Orphée, 264
Orr, Mary, 9
Osborn, Paul, 241, 386
Osborne, John, 352
O'Sullivan, Maurice, 358
Ottieri, Ottiero, 99
Otto e Mezzo, 100
Outcry, The, 144
Ovid, 109

Pagliero, Marcello, 270
Palmer, Frederick, 147
Palmer Handbook of Scenario
  Construction, 147
Parise, Goffredo, 339
Parker, Norton S., 23, 261
Parsons, Louella O., 158, 388
Pascal, Gabriel, 222
Pasolini, Pier Paolo, 252
Pasternak, Boris, 91
Patterson, Frances Taylor, 197,
  200, 303, 378
Paul, Fred, 306
"Paul's Mistress," 231
Pavese, Cesare, 17
Pavlenko, Pyotr, 7, 111
Pearson, Humphrey, 297
Pelissier, Anthony, 102
Pennebaker, D. A., 93
Pépé le Moko, 8
Peple, Edward Henry, 325
Pérez Galdós, Benito, 248
Perilli, Ivo, 33, 41
Perry, Eleanor, 336, 355
Perry, Frank, 336, 355
Perry, George Sessions, 322
Peters, J. M. L., 108, 345
Petronius, 109
Phantom Crown, The, 187
Philippe, Adolphe, 323
Phillips, Gordon, 170
Phillips, Henry Albert, 126, 193,
  263

Photo-Play, The, 217
Photoplay Magazine, 52
Photoplay Scenarios, 157, 186
Photoplay Writing, 63, 224, 371,
  376
Pichel, Irving, 232
Picture Plays and How to Write
  Them, 306
Pinel, Philippe François, 323
Pinelli, Tullio, 43, 92, 100, 191,
  252, 331, 339, 366
Pinero, Arthur Wing, 306
Pirosh, Robert, 316
Place in the Sun, A, 15
Plan for Cinema, 96
Pletnyov, Valeri, 333
Pocock, Roger, 224
Poe, James, 343
Pogson, N. A., 3
Pollack, Sydney, 343
Pollard, Harry A., 348
Ponte della Ghisolfa, Il, 294
Porter, Edwin S., 142, 205
Porter, William Sydney, 338
Potemkin, 35
Powell, Michael, 328
Power, 183
Pratley, Gerald, 226, 387
Pratolini, Vasco, 294
Pratt, George C., 302
Presentation of the Best Films of
  All Time, 77
Pressburger, Emeric, 328
Prévert, Jacques, 73
Professor Unrath, 49
Prosperi, Giorgio, 308
Pulman, Jack, 82
Purcell, Gertrude, 86
Pyle, Ernie, 124

Quarterly of Film, Radio, and
  Television, The, 192, 311
Quatre Cents Coups, Les, 120
Quennell, Peter, 32

Raine, Norman Reilly, 206
Rapf, Maurice, 58
Raphael, Frederic, 359
Rapp, Philip, 382
Rappoport, Herbert, 281
"Rashomon," 267, 288
Rattigan, Terence, 279
Rawlinson, A. R., 125, 183
Ray, Nicholas, 375
Reed, Carol, 108, 259, 345
Reed, R. Ralston, 378
Reference Scenarios, 189
Règle du Jeu, La, 298
Reicher, Frank, 378
Reinhardt, Wolfgang, 187
Reisch, Walter, 253
Reisman, Philip, Jr., 12
Remarque, Erich Maria, 10
Renoir, Jean, 135, 298, 322, 347
Resnais, Alain, 145, 156, 201, 249
Richard, Jean-Louis, 107
Richardson, Jack, 271
Richardson, Tony, 352
Richter, Hans, 101
Rickard, Dick, 320
Riflemen, The, 65
Rise of the American Film, The, 45, 142, 176, 205
Riskin, Robert, 179, 198, 385
Ritt, Martin, 267
Robbe-Grillet, Alain, 201
Roberts, Marguerite, 95
Roberts, Stanley, 62
Robinson, David, 266
Robson, Mark, 68
Rocco e i Suoi Fratelli, 294
Roche, Henri-Pierre, 190
Rolland, Romain, 293
Rondi, Brunello, 92, 100, 109, 191, 339
Rose, William, 199
Ross, Ernest N., 34, 350
Ross, Frank, 242

Rossellini, Roberto, 65, 270
Rosson, Richard, 362
Roth, Philip, 271
Rotha, Paul, 97
Rouverol, Aurania, 215
Royaume de la Terre, Le, 196
Runyon, Damon, 198
Ruskin, Harry, 278
Russell, Robert, 242
Ryskind, Morrie, 246

Salachas, Gilbert, 43, 92, 100, 252, 331
Salacrou, Armand, 38
"Sanatorium," 356
Sanborn, Robert A., 338
Sang d'un Poète, Le, 47
Sargent, Epes Winthrop, 24, 121, 158
Saroyan, William, 164
Sartre, Jean-Paul, 173
Såsom i en Spegel, 349
Satires, 109
Satyricon, 109
Saul, Oscar, 332
Saville, Victor, 233
Saxon, Lyle, 59
Scenario Writing, 34, 350
Scenario Writing Today, 338
Schary, Dore, 329
Schneider, Alan, 113
Schofield, Paul, 369
Schubert, Franz, 48
Schulberg, B. P., 325
Schulberg, Budd, 106, 375
Schulz, Franz, 48
Screen Acting, 116
Screen Writer, The, 232, 382
Screencraft, 40
Screenplay of To Kill a Mockingbird, The, 351
Screenplays of Michelangelo Antonioni, 26, 99, 144, 258

Sears, Ted, 320
Seastrom, Victor, 303
Segal, Alex, 12
Segall, Harry, 154
Seitz, George B., 215, 275, 384
Semprun, Jorge, 145
"Sentinel, The," 360
Sergei Eisenstein, 7, 35, 287
Serpent's Eye, The, 22, 87, 284
Shakespeare, William, 148, 153, 192, 295
Shape of Things to Come, The, 344
Sharman, Maisie, 84
Shavelson, Melville, 382
Shaw, Bernard, 22, 87, 222, 284, 299
Sheekman, Arthur, 382
Sheldon, E. Lloyd, 372
Sherriff, R. C., 134, 241, 259, 286, 356
Sherwin, David, 167
Sherwood, Robert E., 3, 127, 289
Shot Analysis of D. W. Griffith's The Birth of a Nation, A, 45
Shroyer, Frederick B., 286
Shumlin, Herman, 368
Shute, Nevil, 363
"Signal, The," 231
Simon del Desierto, 318
"Sir Tristram Goes West," 127
Sjöman, Vilgot, 165, 166
Sleeping Prince, The, 279
Slesinger, Tess, 133, 354
Slevin, James, 228
Smart, Ralph, 286
Smith, Betty, 354
Smith, David, 116, 338
Smith, Frank Leon, 275
Smith, Robert Paul, 271
Smith, Russell E., 243
Smith, Webb, 320
Smollen, Bradley J., 116

Smultronstället, 373
Solow, Eugene, 260
Solt, Andrew, 184
Sommarnattens Leende, 319
Southern, Terry, 98, 271
Spaak, Charles, 135
Spanish Cavalier, The, 323
Spellbound in Darkness, 302
Spottiswoode, Raymond, 270
"Stage to Lordsburg," 327
Stark, Richard, 219
Stein, Paul L., 48
Steinbeck, John, 119, 137, 232, 260
Sternberg, Josef von, 18, 49, 200, 312
Stevens, George, 242, 276
Stevenson, Philip, 124
Stevenson, Robert, 233
Stevenson, Robert Louis, 36
"Still Life," 55
Stoker, Bram, 257
Stoloff, Benjamin, 353
Storm, Lesley, 108
Strand, Paul, 247
Stroheim, Erich von, 143
Strucchi, Stefano, 227
Struther, Jan, 241
Sturges, Preston, 146, 238
Successful Film Writing, 127
Suetonius, 109
Sullivan, C. Gardner, 59, 147, 302
Suna no Onna, 380
Swindle, The, 43
Synopsis and Continuity of Hail the Woman, 147

Talbot, Daniel, 277
Taradash, Daniel, 122
Tarkington, Booth, 221
Tasker, Robert, 31
Tattoli, Elda, 74
Taurog, Norman, 4

Tavel, Ronald, 149
Taylor, Donald, 89
Taylor, Edward C., 1
Taylor, Stanner E. V., 234
Teaching About the Film, 108, 345
Technique of the Photoplay, The, 24, 121
Templeton, William, 108
Tentazioni del Dottor Antonio, Le, 339
Terriss, Tom, 56, 362, 372
Teshigahara, Hiroshi, 380
Testament d'Orphée, Le, 341
Testori, Giovanni, 294
Theatre Arts, 124, 175
Thoeren, Robert, 321
Thomas, Arthur Winfield, 114, 115, 117, 243, 325
Thomas, Dylan, 36, 89, 265, 290, 358
Thompson, Harlan, 297
Thompson, Robert E., 343
Thorne, Anthony, 32
Three British Screen Plays, 55, 259, 305
"Three Faces of Evil, The," 23
Three Films by Ingmar Bergman, 315, 349, 377
Three Screen Plays (Buñuel), 105, 318, 365
Three Screen Plays (Fellini), 43, 339, 366
Three Screenplays (Visconti), 185, 294, 370
Thunder Over Mexico, 287
Time in the Sun, 287
To Live, 169
Tolstoy, Leo, 19, 20
Tomson, Frederick, 174
Totheroh, Dan, 11, 384
Totò, il Buono, 237
"Tra Donne Sole," 17

Tragedy of the Deportations, The, 249
Transition, 313
Trotti, Lamar, 172, 269, 374
Truffaut, François, 107, 120, 190
Trumbo, Dalton, 346
Turnbull, Margaret, 378
Twain, Mark, 4
Twenty Best Film Plays, 11, 112, 123, 133, 137, 154, 163, 179, 187, 206, 209, 223, 240, 241, 246, 289, 327, 347, 381, 383, 384
Two Screenplays (Cocteau), 47, 341
Two Screenplays (Visconti), 308, 340
Tyler, Charles W., 1
Tystnaden, 315

Unforbidden Fruit, 372
Unger, Gladys, 138

Vadim, Roger, 204
Vailland, Roger, 204
Van, Wallie, 71
Vasiliev, Dmitri, 7
Vávra, Otakar, 181
Veiller, Anthony, 251
"Verger, The," 356
Vidor, Charles, 268
Vidor, King, 76
Viertel, Salka, 19
Visconti, Luchino, 185, 294, 308, 340, 370
Vreeland, Frank, 8, 59, 76, 172, 215, 320, 342, 369, 385, 386

Wagner, Jack, 232
Wald, Jerry, 29, 86, 90, 134, 240, 253, 289
Waldron, Gloria, 296
Walker, Stuart, 138

124

Wallace, Richard, 386
Walsh, Kay, 139
War Is Over, The, 145
Warde, Ernest C., 224
Warfel, Harry R., 16
Warhol, Andy, 51, 149
Washington Square, 152
Watkins, Peter, 367
Watson, William H., 371
Wax, Mo, 104
We Made a Film in Cyprus, 81
"We, the O'Learys," 172
Wead, Frank, 76
Weaver, John V. A., 4, 372
Wegener, Paul, 132
Weinberg, Herman G., 18, 253, 312
Weinstein, Arnold, 271
Welch, Eddie, 369
Welles, Orson, 77, 221
Wellman, William A., 124, 269
Wells, H. G., 195, 225, 344
Welsh, Robert E., 1
Werfel, Franz, 187
West, Claudine, 133, 134, 241
Westerby, Robert, 57
Westlake, Donald E., 219
Weston, Garnett, 297
Weston, Harold, 310
Whately, Roger, 317
White, Lionel, 274
Wickwire, C. J., 361
Wiene, Robert, 61
Wilde, Oscar, 171
Wilder, Billy, 94, 177, 212, 253, 321, 334
Wilhelm, Wolfgang, 307
Willets, Gilson, 168
Williams, Alice, 21
Williams, C. Jay, 21
Williams, Emlyn, 76

Williams, Tennessee, 28, 251, 308, 332
Wilson, Ben, 52
Wilson, Harry Leon, 297
Wilson, Michael, 15, 276, 301
Wimperis, Arthur, 241, 280
"Winds of Change," 23
Windust, Bretaigne, 53
Wing, William E., 114
"Winter Cruise," 102
"Wisdom of Eve, The," 9
"With Clear Rights," 1
With Eisenstein in Hollywood, 15, 335
Wolff, David, 247
Wolff, Friedrich, 281
Wood, Robin, 17
Wood, Sam, 134, 141
Woodhouse, Bruce, 236
Woods, Frank E., 45
Woods, Walter, 263, 335
Wormser, Olga, 249
Wouk, Herman, 62
Wray, John Griffith, 147
Wright, William Lord, 21, 63, 140, 224, 348, 371, 376
Writing for the Screen, 337
Writing the Photoplay, 379
Writing the Sound and Dialogue Photoplay, 56, 362, 372
Wyler, William, 152, 241, 383
Wylie, I. A. R., 386

Years Are So Long, 223
Young, Terence, 32
"Your Arkansas Traveler," 106

Zapponi, Bernardino, 109
Zavattini, Cesare, 42, 237
Zinnemann, Fred, 122
Zola and His Times, 206
Zwerin, Charlotte, 300

THE SERIF SERIES: BIBLIOGRAPHIES AND CHECKLISTS

GENERAL EDITOR: William White, Wayne State University

---

1 *Wilfred Owen (1893-1918): A Bibliography* by William White, with a prefacing note by Harold Owen
SBN: 87338-017-7/ 41pp/ introduction/ preface

2 *Raymond Chandler: A Checklist* by Matthew J. Bruccoli
SBN: 87338-015-0/ ix, 35pp/ introduction

3 *Emily Dickinson, A Bibliography: 1850-1966* by Sheila T. Clendenning
SBN: 87338-016-9/ xxx, 145pp/ preface/ introduction

4 *John Updike: A Bibliography* by C. Clarke Taylor
SBN: 87338-018-5/ vii, 82pp/ introduction

5 *Walt Whitman: A Supplementary Bibliography (1961-1967)* by James T. F. Tanner
SBN: 87338-019-3/ vi, 59pp/ introduction

6 *Erle Stanley Gardner: A Checklist* by E. H. Mundell
SBN: 87338-034-7/ ix, 91pp/ introduction/ indices

7 *Bernard Malamud: An Annotated Checklist* by Rita Nathalie Kosofsky
SBN: 87338-037-1/ xii, 63pp/ preface/ author's note

8 *Samuel Beckett: A Checklist* by J. T. F. Tanner and J. Don Vann
SBN: 87338-051-1/ vi, 85pp/ introduction

9 *Robert G. Ingersoll: A Checklist* by Gordon Stein
SBN: 87338-047-9/ xxx, 128pp/ preface/ introduction/ index

10 *Jean-Paul Sartre in English: A Bibliographical Guide* by Allen J. Belkind
SBN: 87338-049-5/ xx, 234pp/ preface/ introduction/ index

11 *Tolkien Criticism: An Annotated Checklist* by Richard C. West
SBN: 87338-052-5/ xvi, 73pp/ foreword/ title index

12 *Thomas Wolfe: A Checklist* by Elmer D. Johnson
SBN: 87338-050-9/xiv, 278pp/ introduction

13   *A List of the Original Appearances of Dashiell Hammett's Magazine Work* by E. H. Mundell
     SBN: 87338-033-9/ viii, 52pp/ preface

14   *Graham Greene: A Checklist of Criticism*
     by J. Don Vann
     SBN: 87338-101-7/ vii, 69pp/ preface

15   *Theodore Dreiser: A Checklist*
     by Hugh C. Atkinson
     SBN: 87338-048-7/ vii, 104pp/ preface

16   *Richard Wilbur: A Bibliographical Checklist*
     by John P. Field with a note by Richard Wilbur
     SBN: 87338-035-5/ x, 85pp/ note/ introduction

Reference